1st EDITION

Perspectives on Modern World History

The *Exxon Valdez* Oil Spill

1st EDITION

Perspectives on Modern World History

The *Exxon Valdez* Oil Spill

Noah Berlatsky

Editor

GREENHAVEN PRESS
A part of Gale, Cengage Learning

GALE
CENGAGE Learning™

Detroit • New York • San Francisco • New Haven, Conn • Waterville, Maine • London

GALE
CENGAGE Learning™

Elizabeth Des Chenes, *Managing Editor*

© 2011 Greenhaven Press, a part of Gale, Cengage Learning.

Gale and Greenhaven Press are registered trademarks used herein under license.

For more information, contact:
Greenhaven Press
27500 Drake Rd.
Farmington Hills, MI 48331-3535
Or you can visit our Internet site at gale.cengage.com.

For product information and technology assistance, contact us at
Gale Customer Support, 1-800-877-4253.

For permission to use material from this text or product, submit all requests online at
www.cengage.com/permissions.

Further permissions questions can be e-mailed to permissionrequest@cengage.com.

Articles in Greenhaven Press anthologies are often edited for length to meet page requirements. In addition, original titles of these works are changed to clearly present the main thesis and to explicitly indicate the author's opinion. Every effort is made to ensure that Greenhaven Press accurately reflects the original intent of the authors. Every effort has been made to trace the owners of copyrighted material.

Cover image © Natalie Fobes/Corbis.

LIBRARY OF CONGRESS CATALOGING-IN-PUBLICATION DATA
The Exxon Valdez oil spill / Noah Berlatsky, book editor.
    p. cm. -- (Perspectives on modern world history)
    Includes bibliographical references and index.
    ISBN 978-0-7377-5791-0 (hardcover)
1. Oil spills--Environmental aspects--Alaska--Prince William Sound Region. 2. Exxon Valdez (Ship).
3. Tankers--Accidents--Environmental aspects--Alaska--Prince William Sound Region. 4. Oil pollution of the sea--Alaska--Prince William Sound Region. 5. Oil pollution of rivers, harbors, etc.--Alaska--Prince William Sound Region. I. Berlatsky, Noah.
    TD427.P4E9325 2011
    363.738'2097983--dc22
                                                            2011008706

Printed in the United States of America
1 2 3 4 5 6 7 15 14 13 12 11

CONTENTS

on whether the captain, Joseph J. Hazelwood, was drunk at the time of the accident.

Environmental policy researchers at a progressive think tank argue that Exxon fought paying compensation to those affected by the spill. As a result, Exxon continued to reap profits and Prince William Sound remains environmentally damaged twenty years after the spill.

money from Exxon for cleanup efforts, as well as by damage to fisheries. However, Exxon money also had some long-term benefits.

The NOAA says that, sixteen years after the spill, oil from the *Exxon Valdez* has largely dissipated. The ecosystem of Prince William Sound is still disrupted but seems likely to stabilize.

CHAPTER 3   Personal Narratives

FOREWORD

"History cannot give us a program for the future, but it can give us a fuller understanding of ourselves, and of our common humanity, so that we can better face the future."
—Robert Penn Warren,
American poet and novelist

The history of each nation is punctuated by momentous events that represent turning points for that nation, with an impact felt far beyond its borders. These events—displaying the full range of human capabilities, from violence, greed, and ignorance to heroism, courage, and strength—are nearly always complicated and multifaceted. Any student of history faces the challenge of grasping the many strands that constitute such world-changing events as wars, social movements, and environmental disasters. But understanding these significant historic events can be enhanced by exposure to a variety of perspectives, whether of people involved intimately or of ones observing from a distance of miles or years. Understanding can also be increased by learning about the controversies surrounding such events and exploring hot-button issues from multiple angles. Finally, true understanding of important historic events involves knowledge of the events' human impact—of the ways such events affected people in their everyday lives—all over the world.

Perspectives on Modern World History examines global historic events from the twentieth-century onward by presenting analysis and observation from numerous vantage points. Each volume offers high school, early college level, and general interest readers a thematically arranged anthology of previously published materials that address a major historical event, with an emphasis on international coverage. Each volume opens with background information on the event, then presents the controversies surrounding that event, and concludes with first-person narratives from people who lived through the event or were affected by it. By providing primary sources from the time of the event, as well as relevant commentary surrounding the event, this series can be used to inform debate, help develop critical thinking skills, increase global awareness, and enhance an understanding of international perspectives on history.

Material in each volume is selected from a diverse range of sources, including journals, magazines, newspapers, nonfiction books, personal narratives, speeches, congressional testimony, government documents, pamphlets, organization newsletters, and position papers. Articles taken from these sources are carefully edited and introduced to provide context and background. Each volume of Perspectives on Modern World History includes an array of views on events of global significance. Much of the material comes from international sources and from US sources that provide extensive international coverage.

Each volume in the Perspectives on Modern World History series also includes:

- A full-color **world map**, offering context and geographic perspective.
- An annotated **table of contents** that provides a brief summary of each essay in the volume.
- An **introduction** specific to the volume topic.
- For each viewpoint, a brief **introduction** that has notes about the author and source of the viewpoint, and that provides a summary of its main points.
- Full-color **charts**, **graphs**, **maps**, and other visual representations.

- Informational **sidebars** that explore the lives of key individuals, give background on historical events, or explain scientific or technical concepts.
- A **glossary** that defines key terms, as needed.
- A **chronology** of important dates preceding, during, and immediately following the event.
- A **bibliography** of additional books, periodicals, and websites for further research.
- A comprehensive **subject index** that offers access to people, places, and events cited in the text.

Perspectives on Modern World History is designed for a broad spectrum of readers who want to learn more about not only history but also current events, political science, government, international relations, and sociology—students doing research for class assignments or debates, teachers and faculty seeking to supplement course materials, and others wanting to improve their understanding of history. Each volume of Perspectives on Modern World History is designed to illuminate a complicated event, to spark debate, and to show the human perspective behind the world's most significant happenings of recent decades.

INTRODUCTION

On March 24, 1989, the tanker *Exxon Valdez* set out from the marine terminal at Valdez, Alaska, and ran aground in Prince William Sound. In the next few days, the tanker spilled more than 11 million gallons of oil into the sound. The disaster was the worst oil spill in US history up to that time.

The size of the *Exxon Valdez* disaster was unprecedented, but it was not completely unexpected. Before the spill, Alaskans and the people of the United States more broadly had long debated and worried about the effect of large-scale oil extraction and transportation on the economy and environment.

Before the *Exxon Valdez* disaster, much of the discussion about oil in Alaska involved a controversy around drilling in the Arctic National Wildlife Refuge (ANWR). By 1989, conservationists and developers had been struggling for more than a decade over how best to utilize the millions of acres of Alaskan wilderness which were not affected by the Trans-Alaska Pipeline System. Environmental groups wanted to keep the area pristine, while developers argued that the oil in the area should be extracted for economic and national security reasons. M. Lynne Corn and her coauthors summarized the issue in a 2002 article on the website of Almanac of Policy Issues: "The conflict between high oil potential and nearly pristine nature creates a dilemma: should Congress open the area for oil and gas development or should the area's ecosystem be given permanent protection from development?"

In 1986, a draft report by the United States Fish and Wildlife Service recommended "that all of the coastal plain within the Arctic National Wildlife Refuge be opened for oil and gas development," according to Philip Shabecoff in a November 25, 1986, article in the *New York Times*. The article quoted William P. Horn, assistant interior secretary for fish and wildlife in the Ronald Reagan administration, saying that drilling should commence in ANWR because it was "a supergiant oil field that does not exist anywhere else in the United States."

Environmental groups continued to speak against the opening of ANWR. However, by March of 1989 "a bill permitting drilling in the reserve was sailing through the Senate," according to E.J. Dionne in an April 3, 1989, article in the *New York Times*. The bill seemed certain to become law later in the year.

The *Exxon Valdez* disaster, however, interrupted the process. "We hoped before the oil spill to come out with a bill by July," Representative Water B. Jones was quoted as saying in an April 12, 1989, article in the *New York Times*. "But due to the emotional crisis this spill has created, we think it is best to put it on the back burner for the time being until the emotionalism has subsided." In fact, as of 2011, the fate of ANWR remains undecided. The region has not been opened to drilling, but neither has it been permanently closed to development.

ANWR was the focus of attention before the *Exxon Valdez* spill, but many Alaskans and environmental groups had also expressed concerns about the potential dangers posed by oil tankers. These worries were heightened in the months before the *Exxon Valdez* disaster by two oil spills. The first spill involved the ship the *Thompson Pass*, which began leaking oil through an 11-foot crack in its hull on January 3, 1989. It eventually released 71,000 gallons of oil, making it the largest tanker spill in the history of the port of Valdez up to that time. However, according to Patti Epler in a January 5, 1989, article in the *Anchorage Daily News*, unusually clear weather allowed the oil to be "contained in large floating booms that were put around the ship immediately after it

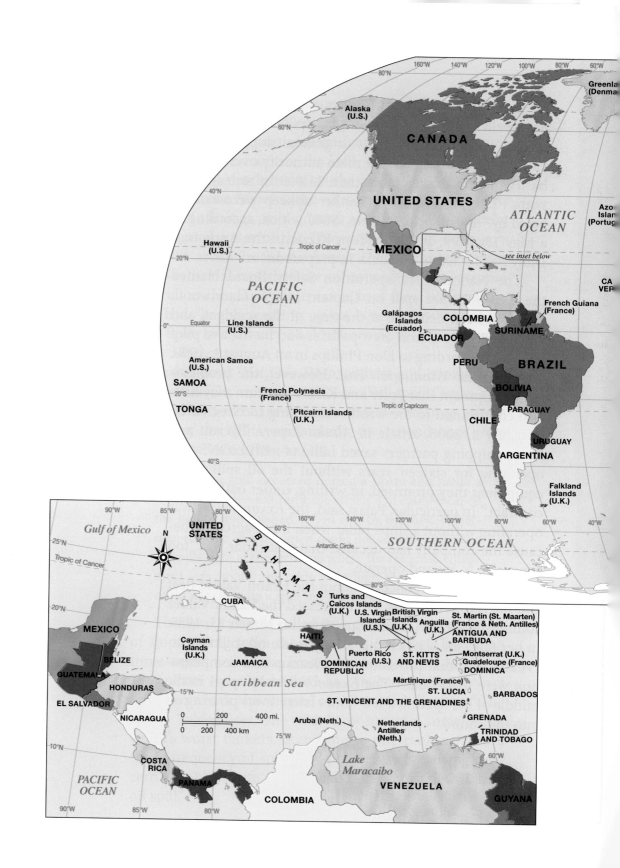

160°W   140°W   120°W   100°W   80°W   60°W

80°N

Greenla
(Denma

Alaska
(U.S.)

CANADA

60°N

40°N

UNITED STATES

ATLANTIC
OCEAN

Azo
Islan
(Portug

Hawaii
(U.S.)

Tropic of Cancer

20°N

MEXICO

see inset below

CA
VER

PACIFIC
OCEAN

Galápagos
Islands
(Ecuador)

COLOMBIA

French Guiana
(France)

Equator   0°

Line Islands
(U.S.)

ECUADOR

SURINAME

PERU

BRAZIL

American Samoa
(U.S.)

20°S

SAMOA

French Polynesia
(France)

BOLIVIA

TONGA

Pitcairn Islands
(U.K.)

Tropic of Capricorn

PARAGUAY

CHILE

URUGUAY

ARGENTINA

40°S

Falkland
Islands
(U.K.)

160°W   140°W   120°W   100°W   80°W   60°W   40°W

60°S

SOUTHERN OCEAN

Antarctic Circle

80°S

90°W   85°W   80°W

Gulf of Mexico

UNITED
STATES

N

25°N

B A H A M A S

Tropic of Cancer

Turks and
Caicos Islands
(U.K.)

CUBA

20°N

U.S. Virgin
Islands
(U.S.)

British Virgin
Islands
(U.K.)

Anguilla
(U.K.)

St. Martin (St. Maarten)
(France & Neth. Antilles)

ANTIGUA AND
BARBUDA

MEXICO

Cayman
Islands
(U.K.)

HAITI

Puerto Rico
(U.S.)

ST. KITTS
AND NEVIS

Montserrat (U.K.)
Guadeloupe (France)
DOMINICA

BELIZE

JAMAICA

DOMINICAN
REPUBLIC

GUATEMALA

Caribbean Sea

Martinique (France)

ST. LUCIA

BARBADOS

HONDURAS

15°N

ST. VINCENT AND THE GRENADINES

EL SALVADOR

GRENADA

NICARAGUA

0   200   400 mi.

75°W

Aruba (Neth.)

Netherlands
Antilles
(Neth.)

TRINIDAD
AND TOBAGO

0   200   400 km

10°N

60°W

COSTA
RICA

PACIFIC
OCEAN

PANAMA

COLOMBIA

Lake
Maracaibo

VENEZUELA

GUYANA

90°W   85°W   80°W

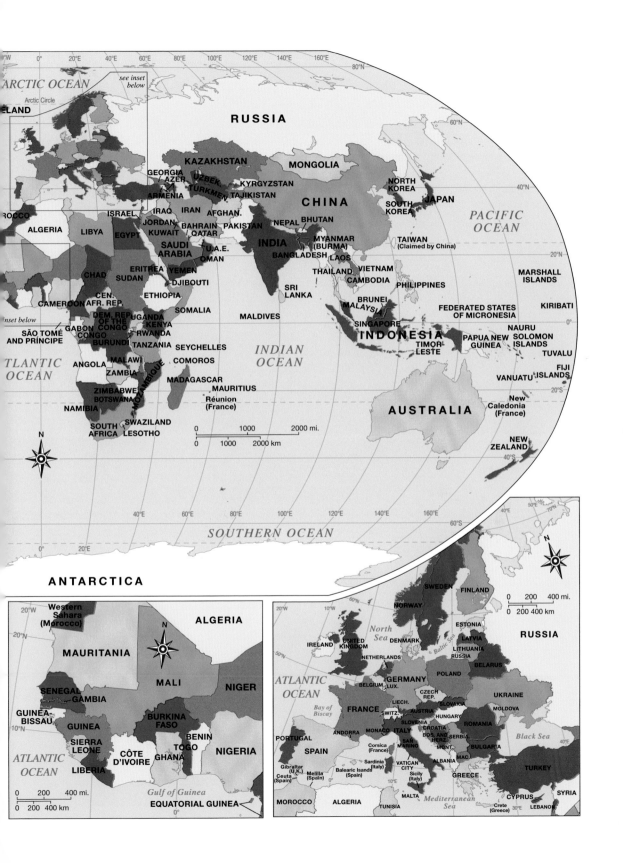

ARCTIC OCEAN

Arctic Circle

ELAND

see inset below

RUSSIA

60°N

KAZAKHSTAN

MONGOLIA

40°N

NORTH KOREA

JAPAN

GEORGIA
AZER.
ARMENIA

UZBEK.
TURKMEN.

KYRGYZSTAN

TAJIKISTAN

CHINA

SOUTH KOREA

PACIFIC OCEAN

ROCCO

IRAQ
ISRAEL
JORDAN
KUWAIT

IRAN
AFGHAN.

PAKISTAN

NEPAL BHUTAN

TAIWAN
(Claimed by China)

ALGERIA

LIBYA

EGYPT

BAHRAIN
QATAR

INDIA

MYANMAR
(BURMA)

20°N

SAUDI ARABIA

U.A.E.
OMAN

BANGLADESH

LAOS

MARSHALL ISLANDS

CHAD

ERITREA YEMEN

THAILAND

VIETNAM

CAMBODIA

PHILIPPINES

SUDAN

DJIBOUTI

SRI LANKA

BRUNEI

CEN. AFR. REP.

ETHIOPIA

SOMALIA

MALAYSIA

FEDERATED STATES OF MICRONESIA

KIRIBATI

CAMEROON

DEM. REP. OF THE CONGO

UGANDA KENYA

MALDIVES

SINGAPORE

NAURU

SOLOMON ISLANDS

0°

GABON CONGO

RWANDA

INDONESIA

PAPUA NEW GUINEA

nset below

SÃO TOMÉ AND PRÍNCIPE

BURUNDI

TANZANIA

SEYCHELLES

TIMOR-LESTE

TUVALU

TLANTIC OCEAN

ANGOLA

MALAWI

ZAMBIA

COMOROS

INDIAN OCEAN

VANUATU

FIJI ISLANDS

20°S

ZIMBABWE

MADAGASCAR

MAURITIUS

AUSTRALIA

New Caledonia (France)

NAMIBIA

BOTSWANA

Réunion (France)

SWAZILAND

SOUTH AFRICA

LESOTHO

0   1000   2000 mi.

0   1000   2000 km

NEW ZEALAND

40°S

N

SOUTHERN OCEAN

ANTARCTICA

SWEDEN FINLAND

0   200   400 mi.

0   200 400 km

NORWAY

Western Sahara (Morocco)

ALGERIA

North Sea

ESTONIA

RUSSIA

IRELAND

DENMARK

LATVIA

UNITED KINGDOM

LITHUANIA

MAURITANIA

NETHERLANDS

RUSSIA

BELARUS

MALI

NIGER

GERMANY

POLAND

SENEGAL

BELGIUM LUX.

CZECH REP.

UKRAINE

GAMBIA

ATLANTIC OCEAN

FRANCE

LIECH.

SLOVAKIA

SWITZ.

AUSTRIA

HUNGARY

MOLDOVA

GUINEA-BISSAU

Bay of Biscay

SLOVENIA

ROMANIA

GUINEA

BURKINA FASO

ANDORRA

MONACO ITALY

CROATIA
BOS. AND HERZ.

SERBIA

Black Sea

BENIN

SAN MARINO

MONT.

BULGARIA

SIERRA LEONE

TOGO

NIGERIA

PORTUGAL

VATICAN CITY

ALBANIA

MAC.

TURKEY

CÔTE D'IVOIRE

GHANA

SPAIN

Corsica (France)

Sardinia (Italy)

Sicily (Italy)

GREECE

LIBERIA

ATLANTIC OCEAN

Gibraltar (U.K.)

Balearic Islands (Spain)

CYPRUS

SYRIA

Ceuta (Spain)

Melilla (Spain)

MALTA

Mediterranean Sea

LEBANON

0   200   400 mi.

0   200 400 km

Gulf of Guinea

EQUATORIAL GUINEA

MOROCCO

ALGERIA

TUNISIA

Crete (Greece)

CHAPTER 1

Background on the *Exxon Valdez* Oil Spill

An Overview of the *Exxon Valdez* Oil Spill

Thomas A. Birkland

The following viewpoint explains how the *Exxon Valdez* oil tanker ran aground in Prince William Sound, Alaska, on March 24, 1989. It notes that the oil from the tanker spilled into the pristine environment of the sound, killing wildlife and mobilizing environmental and fishing groups to demand compensation for cleanup. The viewpoint states that the economic impact of the spill was considerable, while the environmental effects are still being debated. It concludes that the spill inspired significant environmental legislation. Thomas Birkland is a professor of public policy at North Carolina State University. This viewpoint is taken from an encyclopedia on the environment and society which he edited.

Photo on previous page: Rescuers attempt to save an oil-soaked bird, one of thousands affected by the *Exxon Valdez* oil spill on March 24, 1989. (**AP Images/Jack Smith.**)

When the *Exxon Valdez* ran aground in Prince William Sound [PWS], it spilled over 11 million gallons (41.8 million liters) of crude oil, the largest single spill ever released in U.S. coastal waters. The spill occurred late in the evening of March 24, 1989. The ship left Port Valdez, Alaska, under the command of Captain Joseph Hazelwood. After leaving port, the captain left the bridge in charge of a third mate who was not licensed to operate in that particular area of Prince William Sound. The ship, having turned into the inbound shipping lanes to avoid ice from nearby glaciers, was supposed to return to the outbound lanes. For several reasons, including missing navigational markers and failing to disengage the ship's autopilot—the ship turned too late, and, just after midnight Alaska Time, the ship struck Bligh Reef, a well-known navigation hazard.

Environmentalists Are Mobilized

While Exxon and the Alyeska Pipeline Service Company—the firm established to build the trans-Alaska oil pipeline—sought to respond to the spill, the sheer volume of oil was simply too great to be contained. Compounding the problem was Alyeska's failure to maintain oil spill response equipment and material in the area, despite their promises to do so. This was made clear in initial media reports and was confirmed in later investigations; almost immediately after word of the spill reached the world, the news media converged on Prince William Sound, beaming pictures of oiled beaches and wildlife to a shocked and angry public. The spill served to mobilize environmental, fishing, and allied groups in efforts to enact more stringent regulation of oil tankers, and to enhance preparation for oil spills. For many of these interests, the *Exxon Valdez* spill was an event that had long been dreaded, and be-

"The actual environmental effects of the *Exxon Valdez* spill are not fully known.

cause of the impact of the spill on wildlife and fisheries, groups that had been suspicious of each other's motives were brought together in a common cause: anger at Exxon and a desire for some sort of compensation.

In the immediate aftermath of the spill, attempts to contain the oil were minimally successful. Exxon hired contractors who attempted to clean beaches of oil by using absorbent rags, and sometimes using superheated water, which may have done nearly as much damage as the oil itself. Even today [2007], vestiges of the *Exxon Valdez* oil spill can be seen along the rocky beaches of Prince William Sound and south-central Alaska. The actual environmental effects of the *Exxon Valdez* spill are not fully known. Many otters and birds were killed by oil, and the salmon fishery was largely ruined for 1989 because of fears that any catch would be tainted by oil. The salmon have since recovered, but the very important herring fishery has never returned to pre-spill levels, although it is not clear whether the decline in herring was due to the oil spill. The oil spill had obvious socioeconomic consequences. Nearly the entire commercial fishing fleet in Cordova, the main fishing port in PWS, was idled by the spill, and while some fishers were able to lease their boats to Alyeska, many felt personal or community pressure to not take money from Exxon. Estimates of the economic impact of the spill ranged from $6 million to $43 million; longer-term impacts were higher.

> The public policy impact of the spill was significant.

Legislation Is Passed

The public policy impact of the spill was significant. The spill directly broke a 14-year legislative deadlock and triggered the passage of the Oil Pollution Act of 1990 (OPA 90), which provided for increasingly stringent regulation of tankers and other oil facilities. While the

Modern Supertankers: Engineering Triumphs and Environmental Catastrophes

Easily the largest movable man-made objects ever constructed, supertankers were created and designed to meet society's enormous demand for petroleum. From fueling our cars to supplying heat to our homes, supertankers have made it possible for many nations to maintain high standards of living. Although supertankers have facilitated the transportation of enormous amounts of petroleum over thousands of miles, they have also caused some of the largest environmental disasters in history.

The first ocean-going tanker ever constructed was the German-designed *Glückauf*. Launched in 1866 to transport petroleum from the United States to Europe, the *Glückauf* was 300 feet (91 m) long, 37 feet (11 m) wide, carried 2,300 short tons (2,088 metric tons) of oil, and had a cruising speed of about nine knots (17 kph). Today, the *Glückauf* could easily fit into the hold of a supertanker, the largest of which is *Knock Nevis* (formerly *Jahre Viking*), which is over 1,500 feet (457 m) long, 227 feet (69 m) wide, and weighs over 565,000 deadweight tons. *Knock Nevis* is now a permanently moored storage tanker. Indeed, ships this large are no longer even called "supertankers," as that term does not adequately capture their size. Instead, they are called "very large crude carriers" and even "ultra large crude carriers."

Although the development of the modern supertanker was a triumph for the shipbuilding industry and a boon to oil-producing nations, it has had a serious negative side-effect: modern supertankers involved in accidents have caused enormous damage to the environment. It was not very long after the first supertankers were constructed in the early-1960s that disaster struck in a way that the shipbuilding industry had not fully anticipated.

On March 18, 1967, the 118,285 deadweight-ton tanker *Torrey Canyon* went aground on the Seven Stones rocks reef, off the coast of Cornwall, England, spilling nearly 35 million gallons (132 million liters) of crude oil. The resulting oil slick was so vast that

Exxon Valdez spill was spectacular and a key turning point in the history of federal oil spill policy, other large oil spills, such as the Santa Barbara oil well blowout in 1969 and the grounding of the Argo Merchant off Nantucket in 1976, also gained considerable attention, but

some of it spread across the entire English Channel all the way to France, covering over 260 square miles (673 square km). Although the spill took place in the ocean, it is worth noting that just one gallon (3.78 liters) of oil can ruin up to an estimated one million gallons (3.78 million liters) of fresh water—the equivalent of a year's supply of water for 50 people.

Since the *Torrey Canyon*, there have been even larger spills. On March 16, 1978, for example, the tanker *Amoco Cadiz* went aground near Portsall, France, spilling an estimated 65 million gallons (246 million liters) of crude oil. An even larger spill resulted from the July 19, 1979, collision between the tankers *Atlantic Empress* and the *Aegean Captain* off Trinidad and Tobago. It is estimated that an incredible 88 million gallons (333 million liters) of crude oil was spilled as a result of that collision.

Perhaps the most infamous of recent oil spills is that of the *Exxon Valdez*. The spill polluted more than 1,300 miles (2,092 km) of Prince William Sound shoreline and severely degraded the economies of the surrounding fishing communities.

Ultimately, as long as the international demand for petroleum remains high, supertankers will continue to be constructed and likely will become larger. However, as Admiral J. W. Kime, Commandant of the U.S. Coast Guard, stated in testimony before Congress, "As long as there are ships at sea, there will be accidents. We cannot alter that fact. What we can strive to do, what our goal should be, is to insure that these accidents are as infrequent as possible, and that their consequences, to the ship, the personnel onboard, and to the environment, are as harmless as possible."

SOURCE. *"The Advent of Modern Supertankers Facilitates the Transportation of Petroleum and Results in Environmental Catastrophe,"* Science and Its Times, *vol. 7, ed. by Neil Schlager and Josh Lauer. Detroit: Gale, 2009.*

without the same policymaking results. The importance of the *Exxon Valdez* in American politics can be attributed to the general proposition that symbols and images are very powerful in politics. The dominant symbols of the *Exxon Valdez* spill were of oiled otters and birds, the

Supertankers such as the *Exxon Valdez* are the largest movable man-made structures ever built. Many see accidents resulting from such ships as inevitable. (**Time & Life Pictures/Getty Images.**)

soiling of the "pristine Alaskan environment," and the image of a large, uncaring oil company, which employed a drunk tanker captain, spilled oil, and then failed to manage the cleanup. These images and stories focused on Alaska as a wild, pristine "last frontier," and made this event particularly compelling to many people and interest groups.

A particularly important outcome of the *Exxon Valdez* spill is the establishment of citizens' advisory councils under OPA 90. Two Regional Citizens' Advisory Councils (RCACs) were established, for the Cook Inlet Region and Prince William Sound. The RCACs are funded by assessments on the oil industry, and include numerous local interest groups. They have discretionary funds for research projects and have been able to promote policy change involving tanker escort and navigation, weather reporting, and air pollution controls.

Another significant outcome was the establishment of the *Exxon Valdez* Oil Spill Trustee Council, established to guide the spending of the $900 million fine assessed on Exxon for the oil spill as part of an agreement between the federal and state government and by Exxon. A $5 billion civil penalty was imposed on the *Exxon Valdez* in 1994, but the federal district court and the Ninth Circuit Court of Appeals have not yet resolved what the appellate court considers an appropriate figure; it has simply signaled to the lower court that $5 billion is too much. Civil claims continue [as of 2007] 17 years after the spill.

The *Exxon Valdez* Spills Its Oil

Bill McAllister

The following viewpoint, published in the *Washington Post* on the day after the disaster, reports on the confusion following the *Exxon Valdez* spill. Officials identify the spill as the worst environmental disaster in Alaska's history, and state there is little hope that the leak can be plugged to stop the release of oil. Local residents worried that the spill would damage the environment and fisheries, resulting in serious economic damage. The spill confirmed concerns long expressed by environmentalists about the dangers of oil shipping. The author concludes that the disaster may affect the debate about expanding oil drilling in Alaska. Bill McAllister was a reporter for the *Washington Post* and *Linn's Stamp News*.

SOURCE. Bill McAllister, "Millions of Gallons of Oil Spill into Alaskan Sound; Waves Hampering Containment Efforts," *Washington Post*, March 25, 1989. Copyright © 1989 by the Washington Post. Reproduced by permission.

A large oil tanker, reportedly maneuvering to avoid an ice field, struck a reef off Valdez, Alaska, early yesterday [March 24, 1989], releasing more than 11 million gallons of crude oil into one of the nation's most productive and pristine sounds and creating the state's worst oil spill.

The Oil Cannot Be Stopped

Coast Guard officials said that the 987-foot Exxon Valdez had lost more than 10 percent of its 60 million gallons of Alaskan crude oil and that a black plume 1,000 yards wide extended five miles toward the sea in Prince William Sound.

The leak had slowed to a trickle yesterday afternoon, officials said, but they expressed concern last night that the ship might break apart, a hazard that ironically might increase if workers begin transferring oil from the Exxon Valdez to another vessel.

There were no immediate plans to plug the leak. "You really can't stop it from coming out," Coast Guard Lt. Cmdr. James G. Simpson said, citing extensive damage that the tanker apparently incurred when it slid onto a reef 25 miles outside Valdez, the southern terminus of the Trans-Alaska Pipeline.

> Officials were hampered by the remote site of the spill and lack of supplies.

Gov. Steve Cowper (D), interviewed at Valdez airport where he went to view the spill yesterday afternoon, described the accident as "the worst oil spill in Alaska by a long shot" and said it appeared to have been the result of "human error." He declined to elaborate.

Asked whether Alaska had sustained a more serious environmental accident, David Ramseur, a spokesman for Cowper, replied: "Nothing comes to mind."

"If there is any good news, it is that the oil is moving out to open water," Ramseur said. He added, however, that officials were hampered by the remote site of the spill and lack of supplies.

"You need a lot of people and a lot of equipment, and we don't have enough people and equipment," Ramseur said. Officials were using National Guard members in an effort to move pollution-fighting equipment to the site, but a Coast Guard aide said waves were hampering efforts to contain the oil with booms.

Cowper said there was "no way to be prepared" for the accident, although he added, "It's something that people have been expecting for a long time."

Officials also expressed concern about potential damage that millions of gallons of thick, North Slope crude oil would do to the marine-rich sound.

"We're very shocked and concerned," said Chuck Meacham, a regional biologist for the Alaska Department of Fish and Game. "The sound is a very special place in terms of ecology. It has an incredible complex of species that include all five species of salmon, herring, ground [bottom] fish, crab and shrimp."

The Exxon Valdez was reported "hard aground" with a starboard list on Bligh Reef, a submerged shoal marked by a navigational warning light. A second Exxon tanker, the Baton Rouge, came near the crippled ship yesterday afternoon, and officials were considering transferring the Exxon Valdez's remaining cargo, an operation expected to begin this morning.

Coast Guard officials said they were considering using a smaller barge for the transfer because it could maneuver closer to the Exxon Valdez.

Wildlife and Economy Threatened

Gary Kompkoff, president of the community council in the fishing village of Tatitlek about five miles from the accident, said ducks found nearby were covered with the black crude oil. The slick, he said, was nearing islands in the sound.

Most immediately imperiled in the sound is the spring harvest of valuable herring roe, which is prized by Japanese as a delicacy. The harvest is scheduled to begin in early April.

"The grounding has occurred right smack in the middle of the herring . . . operation," Meacham said. "It's very difficult to know what ultimately will happen. The potential for serious problems is just staggering."

> 'This is like getting hit with a 25-ton sledgehammer right now.'

Jack Lamb, vice president of Cordorva District Fishermen's United, said, "This is like getting hit with a 25-ton sledgehammer right now."

Environmentalists recalled difficulties two years ago when Alaskan authorities fought a spill of no more than 200,000 gallons of crude oil in Cook Inlet, another major fishery area, and expressed hope that pollution-control teams were more prepared now.

Kompkoff said many people in his village were puzzled about why the ship appeared to be far from the Valdez commercial shipping channel at the time of the accident about 12:30 A.M. local time [4:30 A.M. EST]. "That's one thing I don't understand," he said. "It is so far from the shipping lane, it doesn't make sense."

Dave Parish, a spokesman in Anchorage for Exxon Shipping Co., the maritime subsidiary of Exxon USA, which owns the ship, described it as the newest tanker in the U.S. fleet.

"We're curious as hell, but we have not pinpointed any cause at this point," Parish said. There appeared to have been no malfunction aboard the 2-year-old ship, which apparently left Valdez for Long Beach, Calif., with a full load of oil, he said.

A Coast Guard spokesman said that icebergs were in the area and that the ship had received permission to move to the left in the northbound shipping lane as it headed south. The ship continued to port and hit the reef.

The site of the wreck is accessible only by helicopter and boat. Exxon, the Coast Guard, and other government agencies were sending pollution teams to fight the spill.

Interior Department spokesman Steven Goldstein said Secretary Manuel Lujan Jr. had given permission "as a last resort" to use chemicals in an effort to disperse the growing oil slick. "We are doing our best to save what we can," Goldstein said.

The sound is home to whales, sea otters, seals and numerous types of commercial fisheries. The fishing season should open in about a month when herring, followed by salmon, begin their annual runs into islands along the coast.

> Environmentalists said the incident appeared to confirm concern voiced more than two decades ago when the federal government opened Alaska's North Slope oil field on the Arctic Ocean to commercial drilling.

The Spill Confirms Concerns

Environmentalists said the incident appeared to confirm concern voiced more than two decades ago when the federal government opened Alaska's North Slope oil field on the Arctic Ocean to commercial drilling.

At that time, opposition to construction of the pipeline focused on suggestions that the pipeline might rupture, spreading crude oil across the fragile Arctic tundra, or that one of the huge oil tankers would split, despoiling rich coastal waters.

Lisa Speer, a scientist with the Natural Resources Defense Council in New York, said the accident would be cited by opponents of expanding Alaskan oil drilling to include the Arctic National Wildlife Refuge, a large federal reservation east of the oil-rich North Slope.

Earlier this month, the Senate Energy Committee voted, 12 to 7, in favor of a proposal to allow drilling in the refuge.

Photo on previous pages: Within one day of the grounding of the *Exxon Valdez* in Prince William Sound, a black plume of crude oil stretched one thousand yards toward the sea. (**National Geographic/Getty Images.**)

Petroleum companies have planned to add a leg to the pipeline and ship oil from the refuge to Valdez. Opposition has not focused on the hazards of shipping by tanker, but Speer and other environmentalists said they would raise those issues during hearings in the House.

"This is an important issue that has been ignored thus far," she said, citing what an Anchorage newspaper has described as an increasing number of pollution incidents at Valdez.

Coast Guard officials closed the port of Valdez to commercial shipping. And the National Transportation Safety Board began investigating the accident.

Alaska Undertakes a Criminal Investigation into the *Exxon Valdez* Spill

David Postman, George Frost, and David Hulen

In the following viewpoint from the week after the spill, an Alaskan newspaper reports that the state has launched a criminal investigation into the disaster. The investigation focuses on the question of whether the *Exxon Valdez* captain, Joseph J. Hazelwood, was drunk at the time of the accident. An investigation of Gregory T. Cousins, the third mate who was steering the ship when it grounded, is also being conducted. In addition, investigators are looking into the possibility of litigation against Alyeska Pipeline, which is responsible for the cleanup, and Exxon itself. David Postman, George Frost, and David Hulen were all reporters for the *Anchorage Daily News* at the time of the spill.

Anchorage—The state has opened a criminal investigation to determine whether anyone involved in the grounding of the tanker Exxon Valdez should face prosecution, Gov. Steve Cowper said Tuesday.

Charges of Drunkenness

Cowper said the state's investigation into the disastrous spill of 11 million gallons of oil last Friday [March 24, 1989] into Prince William Sound will parallel the inquiry already under way by investigators of the National Transportation Safety Board [NTSB], who spent the day interviewing officers of the Valdez including its captain, Joseph J. Hazelwood.

"The NTSB's purpose is to find out why the accident happened and to make sure it doesn't happen again," said Cowper, who is also a lawyer. "They don't investigate criminal charges."

Garrey Peska, Cowper's chief of staff, said the NTSB has so far refused a state request to share its copies of the ship's logs, charts and licenses of its officers.

> The criminal investigation has centered on the sobriety and state of mind of Capt. Hazelwood.

"The NTSB told us they were too busy," Peska said on board the plane that was carrying him, Cowper and other officials to Valdez. "Right now, we're going to help them find a little free time."

Attorney General Doug Baily said the criminal investigation has centered on the sobriety and state of mind of Capt. Hazelwood, who turned over the bridge of the Exxon Valdez to the ship's third mate, Gregory T. Cousins.

According to the Coast Guard and Exxon, Cousins was unlicensed to command the vessel through Prince William Sound. The ship was under Cousins' command when it veered off course, into the area of rocky reefs.

The ship struck one rock, and two miles later grounded on another, Exxon has said.

Earlier this week, Alaska Public Safety Director Art English said that the Coast Guard asked a state trooper to check out a report that Hazelwood had been drinking.

"On the basis of any evidence we have been able to run out, there are no witnesses saying he was drunk or impaired by drugs or alcohol," Baily said. "I'd say something about his performance was impaired or he would not have had another man at the conn [controls] in his place," he said.

Searching for Witnesses

Among the witnesses who have given statements are the senior crew members on watch that night, and a pilot who was on board to guide the Valdez from the terminal to Rocky Point, according to Baily.

"The pilot is one of the key people," Baily said. "We would be more inclined to rely on the testimony of somebody who is not a subordinate to the captain."

> If no witnesses are found who can testify to obvious signs of impairment, 'then all that's left is the blood test.'

According to Baily, Hazelwood denied in interviews with Coast Guard investigators that he was intoxicated that night, but Baily said he has not been privy to all the reports compiled by the Coast Guard and the NTSB, which conducted further interviews Tuesday.

English said that troopers have not talked to the captain yet.

"We are trying to see the steps of the crew before they got aboard, and talk to the people who may have had contact with the crew," he said. Investigators are interviewing dock workers, cab drivers, bartenders and others.

If no witnesses are found who can testify to obvious signs of impairment, "then all that's left is the blood test,"

The Captain Is Vilified

When Captain Joseph Hazelwood heads for the mailbox these days, he no longer waves to his neighbors in Huntington Bay, N.Y. Instead, his head sagging, he hurries back indoors to the lonely anguish that has engulfed his life since the early morning of March 24 [1989], when his tanker, the *Exxon Valdez*, struck a reef in Alaska's Prince William Sound and leaked 11 million gal. of crude oil into the pristine waters.

Since then, Hazelwood has been a man under siege. Not long after the accident, a TV reporter beat him to the mailbox and rifled through his letters until neighbors chased her away. Other journalists have surrounded his home, flashing cameras through windows and banging on doors. Still others have stolen bags of garbage from the curb. Then there are the sneers of strangers, the steady stream of Hazelwood songs and jokes, the death threats to his family from anonymous callers, some of whom promise to blow the pretty yellow house to smithereens. Whatever respite Hazelwood may have enjoyed as the story faded from the front pages probably ended last week, when the crippled *Exxon Valdez*, on its way for repairs, caused an 18-mile-long oil slick off San Diego. Suddenly the tanker was thrust back into the headlines.

Fired from Exxon in March in the wake of the Alaska disaster, Hazelwood, 42, is discovering how America treats those it deems to be villains. Newspapers and late-night comics had a field day with early press reports depicting a boozy Hazelwood leaving the bridge of the 987-ft. tanker and turning control over to an unqualified mate. SKIPPER WAS DRUNK, screamed the *New York Post*. "I was just trying to scrape some ice off the reef for my margarita," chortled comedian David Letterman, suggesting one of Hazelwood's "Top Ten Excuses" for the spill.

SOURCE. *"Exxon Valdez: Joe's Bad Trip," Time, July 24, 1989.*

Baily said. "If it's zero there is nothing to extrapolate back from."

Medical experts told the *Daily News* that too much time may have elapsed between the time of the accident and the administration of a blood test for any scientific calculation of Hazelwood's alcohol level at the time of the accident. A test was not administered until 8 A.M., according to the Coast Guard. English said the trooper who witnessed the test reported it took place at least two hours after the Coast Guard said.

New York motor vehicle and arrest records show a five year history of alcohol problems on the part of the skipper. His drivers' license has been suspended or revoked three times since 1984, and it was under revocation when he boarded the ship Friday evening.

Cousins also has had driving problems, according to Florida records, and he, too, may lose his license if he doesn't pay a $130 reckless driving fine by April 3.

Records from Tampa, Fla., show that a Mississippi trooper stopped a 1986 Chevrolet Celebrity driven by a Gregory Thomas Cousins from Tampa, Fla., doing 90 miles an hour down Interstate 10 last year. A woman who lives at the same address as the man listed on the violation told a reporter that third mate Cousins was her husband.

When Cousins failed to show for an Aug. 22 court date or pay a fine, Mississippi notified authorities in Florida, who have said they will revoke his license if the fine is not paid by next week.

Corporate Culpability

Baily said a team of civil attorneys has also set up offices in Valdez to gather information about the cause of the spill, the effectiveness of the cleanup and the culpability of Alyeska Pipeline and Exxon for environmental damage caused by the millions of gallons of oil loosed in Prince William Sound.

Alyeska was responsible for implementing a cleanup plan during the first few critical hours of the spill.

> Alyeska was responsible for implementing a cleanup plan during the first few critical hours of the spill. . . . State officials have criticized that effort as too little, too late.

Cowper and other state officials have criticized that effort as too little, too late. Exxon also may be at fault.

Baily said a lawsuit against Exxon or Alyeska Pipeline is not planned at this time. But the state wants to put together information that would "have a rapid handle on it for the purpose of litigation."

"With or without litigation the purpose is to establish environmental baselines, so any alleged losses can be compared to some starting point," he said.

Depending upon the claims of Prince William Sound fishermen, whose $90 million annual fishery is at stake, the state also could seek damages up to $100 million through the transAlaska pipeline (TAPS) liability fund, an oil-industry-financed pot of money set aside for a spill.

Under a TAPS settlement, Exxon would pay the first $14 million and the liability fund would pay claims for the next $86 million. Although parties claiming damages

The National Transportation Safety Board's investigation of the March 24, 1989, oil spill centered on Captain Joseph J. Hazelwood (center) and on allegations that he had been drinking alcohol prior to the spill. **(AP Images/Alan Greth.)**

need not prove fault, only damages, Exxon's total liability is limited to $100 million unless gross negligence led to the disaster.

Baily said a civil suit probably would not include a claim for punitive damages beyond the $100 million, unless it could be shown that Exxon, its crew members or other responsible parties were guilty of "outrageous conduct" that demonstrated a total disregard for the safety of the vessel or the subsequent attempts to contain and clean up the spill.

Looking for the Cause of the Accident

The NTSB investigators spent much of the day interviewing Capt. Hazelwood and Third Mate Cousins. Each officer was accompanied by a lawyer, and would not talk about the shipwreck when asked by reporters.

Hazelwood and Cousins both were to appear before the NTSB on Monday, but did not because their lawyers weren't able to make it here from Anchorage, said William Woody, head of the safety board's team. Exxon officials have said the company was hiring an attorney for Hazelwood, but a company spokeswoman would not say Tuesday who the lawyer was or whether the company was hiring lawyers for Cousins and other crewmen being questioned.

Exxon and Coast Guard officials have said repeatedly that they do not know why Hazelwood left Cousins on watch and William Woody, the chief of the four-man NTSB team, would not comment about what he's learned.

As in airplane crashes, the safety board's role is to determine the cause of the shipwreck. Once evidence is collected here, including sworn testimony from witnesses, the board will conduct a public hearing in Anchorage and, eventually, issue a report with recommendations.

Aside from what went wrong on the ship, the NTSB probe also will look at actions by ship controllers in the

Coast Guard's Vessel Traffic Center and at the way the cleanup has been handled, said Drucella Anderson, a spokeswoman for the NTSB in Washington.

The team consists of three marine investigators and a "human performance investigator," a person NTSB officials say is trained in psychology and looks into things such as fatigue and substance abuse. The team here is the agency's only marine accident group.

The Coast Guard is assisting the NTSB in the investigation, including gathering evidence. Once an investigation is over, the Coast Guard may suspend a vessel or a crewman's license, and if warranted, information can [be] forwarded to the U.S. attorney for criminal prosecution, a Coast Guard spokesman said.

The *Exxon Valdez* Spill May Threaten Canada

Winnipeg Free Press

In the weeks after the spill, a Canadian newspaper reports that the oil slick from the *Exxon Valdez* is closer to the Canadian coast than the Canadian government has admitted. The paper reports that some members of Parliament feel that Canada needs to react more aggressively to the danger. In particular, the opposition wants the government to coordinate more closely with the US president to organize cleanup efforts. The paper notes that the Canadian government itself says that it has responded to the spill adequately and forcefully.

The oil slick released from the Exxon Valdez is much closer to Canada's West Coast than the government is admitting, Jim Fulton, the NDP environment critic [the member of the opposition New Democratic Party of Canada charged with environmen-

---

SOURCE. "MP Raises Alarm Over Oil Spill Slick," *Winnipeg Free Press*, 1989. Copyright © 1989 Winnipeg Free Press. All rights reserved. Reproduced by permission.

tal policy] said yesterday [April 4, 1989] during a rare emergency debate in the Commons.

The Slick Is Spreading

The thick, black slick, which is now half the size of Nova Scotia, is slightly more than 300 kilometres from northwestern British Columbia, not 1,000 kilometres away, said Fulton, who got his information from the Canadian coast guard.

"The mouth of the Alsec River is 209 miles (320 kilometres) from where the slick is, as it comes out of Montague Sound," Fulton said.

"Some gerbil somewhere decided: 'Let's keep the people calm, tell them it's so far away . . . nobody need worry about it.'"

Fulton's riding [electoral district] of Skeena includes the Queen Charlotte Islands and Canadian mainland closest to the Alaskan coast.

However, Tom Siddon, minister of fisheries and oceans, said the slick was moving in a southwesterly direction, away from Canadian shorelines, and called Fulton's allegations irresponsible.

"It is highly improbable that this oil slick will move in that direction towards the Alsec River," Siddon said.

But a shift in wind has already occurred and if a northwesterly wind continues, it could threaten British Columbia shores, Fulton said.

> Liberal Leader John Turner slammed the government for not rushing Canadian scientists to Alaska immediately after the spill occurred to determine what the threat to Canadian waters might be.

Such a shift in the wind is highly unlikely, Siddon said, but he acknowledged that Canadian salmon stocks may face some long-term damage as a result of the oil spill.

Some salmon in the area of the spill return to Canadian waters after spawning in Alaskan rivers.

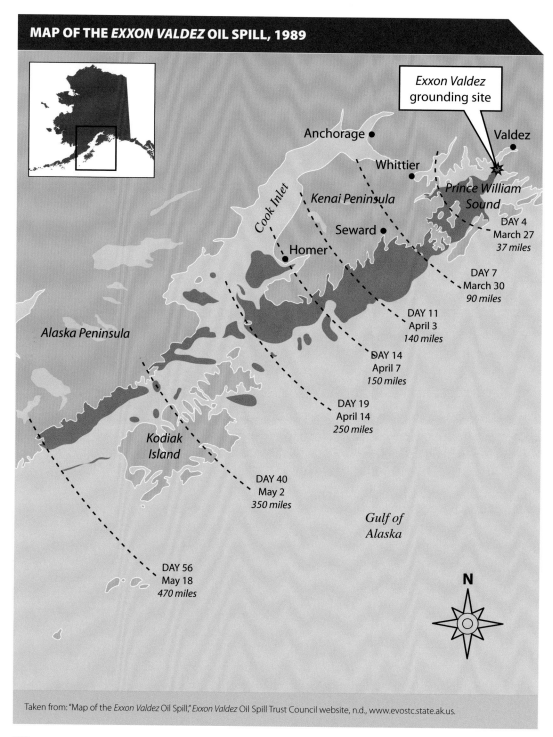

MAP OF THE *EXXON VALDEZ* OIL SPILL, 1989

Exxon Valdez grounding site

Anchorage ●

Valdez ●

Whittier ●

Prince William Sound

Cook Inlet

Kenai Peninsula

Seward ●

Homer ●

DAY 4
March 27
37 miles

DAY 7
March 30
90 miles

DAY 11
April 3
140 miles

DAY 14
April 7
150 miles

DAY 19
April 14
250 miles

Alaska Peninsula

Kodiak Island

DAY 40
May 2
350 miles

Gulf of Alaska

DAY 56
May 18
470 miles

N

Taken from: "Map of the *Exxon Valdez* Oil Spill," *Exxon Valdez* Oil Spill Trust Council website, n.d., www.evostc.state.ak.us.

Canadian halibut stocks could also be threatened if the oil remains in the Gulf of Alaska for an extended period, Siddon said, but it will take months to determine it this threat is real.

Millions of Litres of Oil

More than 40 million litres of crude oil began seeping out of the American supertanker Exxon Valdez on March 24 [1989] when it ran aground near the Alaskan port of Valdez.

Exxon crews finished pumping the remaining crude oil out of the tanker yesterday in preparation for refloating it. The oil spill has floated over about 4,250 square kilometres and soiled 1,300 kilometres of beach. Thousands of animals are known dead, including at least 30 sea otters.

Liberal Leader John Turner slammed the government for not rushing Canadian scientists to Alaska immediately after the spill occurred to determine what the threat to Canadian waters might be.

He also asked Prime Minister [Brian] Mulroney to urge U.S. President [George H.W.] Bush that both countries fight the slick together.

"It's time for the prime minister to call his friend Mr. Bush and say: 'We have to co-ordinate our efforts,'" Turner said.

Environment Minister Lucien Bouchard said the Canadian government reacted as quickly as possible to the dangers posed by the oil spill, but the government's plan to deal with spills will be reviewed and changed if necessary.

Shortly after the *Exxon Valdez* oil spill, Canadian officials debated the potential effects on fish populations such as the sockeye salmon, which inhabit British Columbia's rivers. **(National Geographic/Getty Images.)**

"If we find out that we must upgrade equipment (or) we must improve the swiftness of the reaction time, we will do it and we will report to the public, Bouchard said. "We have nothing to hide."

The *Exxon Valdez* Spill Affects the Environment and the Economy

Samuel K. Skinner and William K. Reilly

The following viewpoint is from the report by the National Response Team prepared for President George H.W. Bush two months after the *Exxon Valdez* disaster. The report notes that Prince William Sound, where the spill occurred, is a very delicate environment. It suggests that the spill will damage birds, marine mammals, and fisheries in both the short and long term. It also predicts economic losses to the fishing industry, to the tourism and recreation industries, and to native villages. The authors recommend putting mechanisms in place to ensure quicker responses to the potential environmental and economic damage caused by future spills. Samuel K. Skinner was the US secretary of transportation at the time of the *Valdez* spill, and William K. Reilly was the administrator of the Environmental Protection Agency.

SOURCE. Samuel K. Skinner and William K. Reilly, *The Exxon Valdez Oil Spill: A Report to the President*, 1989. Copyright © 1989 The National Response Team. All rights reserved. Reproduced by permission.

It still is much too early to know the full extent of the environmental, economic, and health effects of the oil that spilled from the *Exxon Valdez* into the waters off Alaska's south-central coast. The discussion below, which describes these effects, should be regarded as preliminary.

The severity of oil spill effects on the environment varies greatly, depending on the conditions of the spill. The type and amount of oil involved, its degree of weathering, geographic location, seasonal timing, types of habitat affected, sensitivity of the affected organism's life stage, and adequacy of the response all influence the severity of environmental effects. Many of the conditions present during the *Exxon Valdez* spill increased, rather than diminished, the severity of its impacts relative to other large spills. The spill occurred at a high latitude in a semi-enclosed body of water at the beginning of spring. The 10.1 million gallons of oil spilled from the *Exxon Valdez* are known to have oiled over 350 miles of shoreline in Prince William Sound alone. The figure will increase as other affected areas are surveyed.

> The 10.1 million gallons of oil spilled from the *Exxon Valdez* are known to have oiled over 350 million miles of shoreline in Prince William Sound alone.

Prince William Sound Is a Sensitive Environment

In contrast, only 240 miles of coastline were affected by the Amoco Cadiz oil spill in 1978. The Amoco Cadiz released 68 million gallons of oil when it broke up on the rocks in stormy seas off France's Brittany coast. Most of the elements of Brittany's temperate zone environment largely recovered within three to eight years from the effects of the oil spill and ensuing clean-up operations. The habitats of the south-central Alaskan coast generally are more vulnerable to spilled oil than those of more temperate climates because the lower temperatures and resulting slower rates of physical weathering and biodegradation allow the oil to persist. This persistence provides the potential for long-term exposures and sub-lethal chronic effects, as well as short-term exposures and acute effects. In addition, the remoteness of the affected Alaskan area and the physical features of its coastline make cleanup more difficult than it was in Brittany. Great care must be taken in the *Exxon Valdez* cleanup to minimize harm to sensitive environments.

Prince William Sound, the site of the *Exxon Valdez* spill, is one of the largest tidal estuarine systems on the North American continent. In terms of water surface alone, it is about as large as Chesapeake Bay. Its many islands, bays, and fjords give it a shoreline totalling more than 2,000 miles, nearly one-quarter of Chesapeake Bay's total shoreline. Prince William Sound is within the boundaries of the Chugach National Forest. The western half of the sound, the area most affected by the oil spill, is within the Nellie Juan-College Fjord Wilderness study area. This area is highly sensitive environmentally.

Patches of oil or oil-and-water emulsion (mousse) now have moved with the prevailing winds and currents in a southwesterly direction more than 250 miles from the accident site on Bligh Reef. The oil has moved out of Prince William Sound into the Gulf of Alaska and along the Kenai Peninsula and the Kenai Fjords National Park to the islands of Lower Cook Inlet and the Kodiak Archipelago. There is no evidence to date that large quantities of oil have entered the water column or sunk to the bottom in Prince William Sound.

Much of this entire area was largely pristine until the *Exxon Valdez* incident. It is an area of great natural beauty, and its rich natural resources form the basis for major commercial fisheries for pink and chum salmon and Pacific herring. There are smaller fisheries for halibut, sablefish, king, Tanner and Dungeness crabs, and shrimp. The Chugach National Forest in Prince William Sound and Kenai Fjords National Park are relatively accessible by air and boat from Anchorage, the major population center in Alaska, making the area a favorite location for recreational users. The sound is the major food source for the Alaskan Native villages on its shore.

Effects on Birds and Mammals

Immediate spill effects were most visible on marine birds and sea otters. These effects are becoming much less severe as the oil breaks up into smaller patches and, finally, into weathered tar balls.

The bird population of Prince William Sound and the Kenai/Kodiak area is diverse and abundant. The Fish and Wildlife Service (FWS) counted more than 91,000 waterbirds (mostly diving ducks, grebes, and loons) in the sound immediately after the spill. About half of these

The post-spill report to President George H.W. Bush described Prince William Sound—where the town of Cordova, Alaska, is located—as an area of pristine natural beauty and significant wildlife populations. (AP Images/Al Grillo.)

birds were in or near areas affected by floating oil. As the spring migration gets underway, large numbers of waterfowl and shorebirds that stop to feed in the Prince William Sound area potentially could be exposed to the spilled oil. Many of these birds may be affected either directly by oil or indirectly through the loss of food sources.

As the oil moves along the Kenai Peninsula and the Kodiak Archipelago, it will continue to affect shorebirds and waterfowl. The severity of the impact will depend on the amount of oil that reaches these areas, its degree of weathering and emulsification, and how long it persists near the seabird colonies. Seabirds are just beginning to occupy colonies for this year's breeding season. The success of this breeding season also could be diminished because of habitat loss, loss of food resources, and mortality of chicks and eggs. Oil transferred from the feathers of brooding birds is toxic to embryos within the eggs. For the reasons discussed above and because of the difficulty in recovering bodies, the 4,463 dead birds collected do not represent the full toll.

Twenty-three species of marine mammals live in the sound and the Gulf of Alaska either year-round or during the summer. These mammals include gray, humpback, and killer whales, various porpoises and dolphins, harbor seals, sea lions, and sea otters. Of these animals, the sea otters are by far the most sensitive and vulnerable to spilled oil. Because they are dependent upon fur for insulation, they die of hypothermia and stress when it comes in contact with oil. Fumes from the floating oil also may have contributed to their deaths. As many as 2,500 of Prince William Sound's estimated pre-spill population of 8,000 to 10,000 sea otters are in the western portions of the sound where they may be exposed to oil from the *Exxon Valdez*. The number of dead, currently at 479, is not regarded as an accurate measure of the spill's impact on sea otters because of the difficulty in recovering their bodies. No estimates of total mortality yet have been made.

Other sea otter populations potentially at risk as the oil moves through the Gulf of Alaska off the Kenai Peninsula and the Kodiak Archipelago are the estimated 2,500 to 3,500 otters along the peninsula and the estimated 4,000 to 6,000 around Kodiak and other nearby islands. No other marine mammal (e.g., dolphin, seal, or whale) mortality yet has been attributed to the oil spill, but harbor seals will start pupping in May [1989]. There is concern that oil remaining in harbor seal pupping areas could injure or kill the pups. Priority is being given to cleanup of these areas, but the work must proceed cautiously in order to minimize stress on the pregnant females at this critical time: Terrestrial animals, such as river otters, mink, bald eagles, bear, and deer, that utilize intertidal areas also may be affected through scavenging of oiled carcasses on the beaches or browsing on oiled kelp.

Marine Resources

Oil can affect microscopic plants and animals (phytoplankton and zooplankton) adversely. The latter include the floating eggs and larvae of fish that form the base of the marine food chain. In the open waters of the sound and gulf, this impact probably will be short-lived and local because of the quick replacement of plankton by the same organisms from unaffected areas. For some species, however, mortality of planktonic eggs and larvae may be reflected in long-term population effects. Intertidal animals such as barnacles and mussels, which live in a highly variable and stressful environment, have little or no mobility. Oil in many intertidal areas within Prince William Sound and

> The potential exists for oil released in the *Exxon Valdez* spill to persist in and on parts of this coastline for many years.

elsewhere will result in severe mortality among these animals. Recovery of their populations may take several years.

As the oil from the *Exxon Valdez* moves into the deeply indented coast by means of tidal and wind action, it will affect increasingly sensitive environments. Higher-risk, lower-energy environments are located deeper in fjords and bays. In high-energy environments, such as the headlands along the Kenai Peninsula, wave action tends to remove what oil is stranded rather quickly. In low-energy environments, such as shallow bays and marshes, oil may remain for years with only slow chemical and biological processes to degrade it. The stranded oil will serve as a reservoir for the chronic input of oil into the subtidal sediments, where it may affect bottom dwelling (benthic) organisms over the long term. The potential exists for oil released in the *Exxon Valdez* spill to persist in and on parts of this coastline for many years.

Long-Term Effects on Fisheries

Long-term effects to the area's rich biota may result from food chain and habitat disruption as well as from decreased survivability and reproductive capability of animals directly exposed to oil. Determining these impacts will require study of the species of concern throughout their life cycle or longer. For example, pink salmon have the shortest life cycle among the five different salmon found in the area. These salmon return to spawn two years after their eggs are laid. Prince William Sound alone accounts for 50 percent of Alaska's total commercial harvest of the species.

A series of state and private hatcheries, two of which are the world's largest, support the pink salmon fishery. Hatchery-raised fry normally are released in early April and spend up to three months feeding and growing in the shallow, near-shore areas of the sound before migrating into the Gulf of Alaska. The fate of this year's fry, estimated to exceed 650 million, is a cause for concern. The fry may be killed by hydrocarbons in their nursery areas (they are sensitive to very low concentrations in the water column). Their growth rate may be slower this year due to stress from hydrocarbons or a decrease in the amount of available food. Because smaller fish are more susceptible to predation, fewer adult fish may return in 1991.

Another economically significant long-term effect could be the possible loss of this year's young herring from the affected areas. Pacific herring are second in importance only to salmon among the fishery resources of the area. Their roe (eggs) provide one of the state's most valuable fish products per unit of weight. The herring and roe fishery in Prince William Sound has been closed this year, and restrictions have been placed on the herring fishery off Kodiak because of the spill. Herring are spring (April-May) intertidal and subtidal spawners. They do not spawn until they are at least three years old and return each year thereafter during their life span to spawn in their natal areas.

Herring eggs can cover many miles of the intertidal zone. They are both vulnerable and sensitive to oil. The eggs may be smothered and die outright, or oil may cause developmental abnormalities in the growing embryos. The persistence of stranded oil in herring spawning areas may affect not just the 1989-year class but also subsequent-year classes. This impact can be determined best by examining the spawning adults at areas of impact in 1992, 1993, and 1994 for the percentage of the population recruited from spawn in 1989 through 1991. . . .

Early Lessons Learned/Recommendations

- The Departments of Agriculture, Commerce, and the Interior, as federal Trustees for the affected natural resources, should work closely with the state trustee agency, the Alaska Department of Fish and Game, to plan and implement natural resource damage assessments as quickly as possible. In doing so, they should coordinate their activities with response authorities to avoid interfering with the cleanup.

> In future spills, damage assessment and funding options should be identified quickly.

- The Trustees, together with EPA [Environmental Protection Agency], should work in coordination with the parties assessing long-term environmental effects to avoid duplication and develop the best possible scientific basis for restoration of Prince William Sound and other affected areas.

- Where applicable, results of past studies should be used. New research should be used to confirm earlier preliminary findings *or* to fill gaps.

- In future spills, damage assessment and restoration should begin immediately and funding options should be identified quickly.

- To facilitate response to future incidents, federal Trustee agencies should develop an automatic mechanism to resolve in advance such issues as identification of lead Trustee, management of assessment funding, delineation of restoration responsibilities, and the allocation of restored funds recovered from joint claims.

- Federal agency damage assessment capabilities should be strengthened so that a small cadre of trained and experienced personnel will be able to go immediately to the scene of major spills in the future. . . .

- Wildlife rescue efforts need to be implemented immediately after a spill is reported. In addition, research procedures should be established quickly to allow data collection required to develop improved rescue efforts in the future. . . .

Commercial Fisheries and Recreation

The natural resources of the areas affected by the *Exxon Valdez* spill are important to Alaska's local and statewide economy. While it is too early to know the full extent of the economic consequences of the spill, the local and state economies are likely to suffer economic losses. . . .

Prince William Sound possesses rich commercial fisheries for Pacific herring and salmon, along with smaller halibut, sablefish, crab, and shrimp fisheries. These fisheries are used on a permit basis by commercial fishermen from as far away as Anchorage and Seattle. The Alaskan fishing ports nearest the sound are Cordova, Seward, Homer, and Kodiak. Cordova, probably the most affected of the fishing ports, is the third largest in Alaska and the ninth largest in the United States in terms of the dollar value of commercial fishery landings. Kodiak is the largest Alaskan fishing port and the second largest in the United States.

Together, these two ports had commercial fishery landings of all species valued at $174 million in 1957. This catch represented over 18 percent of the total for Alaska and nearly six percent for the United States in that year. An estimated one-third of Alaska's nearly 12,000 full- or part-time fishermen in 1987 worked in the area now affected by the spill.

Prince William Sound's herring and herring roe fishery (valued at $14 million in 1988) usually opens in early April. Out of concern for additional harm to the stocks and possible contamination of the product, the Alaska Department of Fish and Game closed the herring fishery after the spill and recently restricted part of the herring fishery off Kodiak. It is unknown at this time whether or not the $33-million pink salmon fishery in the sound, which reaches its peak in July and August, will be closed or restricted for similar reasons.

Closings or restrictions *will* harm not only fishermen but also the area's important fish processing industry.

This industry employs an estimated 3,000 to 4,000 people annually. The State of Alaska, with technical assistance from the Food and Drug Administration (FDA), is taking precautions to assure that oil-tainted fish products do not reach the market. The state is assigning 40 extra inspectors to the processing plants serving the affected area and will continue to close fisheries, if necessary, to protect the public. If, despite these measures, consumers avoid Alaskan fish products, the national prices for those products may be depressed temporarily.

> Fishermen in the affected area remain deeply concerned not only about their long-term economic prospects, but also about possible changes in their way of life.

With the spill still spreading, the full economic impact on commercial fishermen is unknown. The immediate economic losses of many local fishermen are being mitigated by their employment in Exxon's clean-up efforts. Fishermen in the affected area remain deeply concerned not only about their long-term economic prospects, but also about possible changes in their way of life.

Recreation and tourism have been increasing rapidly in Prince William Sound over the last 10 years. In the late 1970's, cruise ships did not visit the sound, but, by 1987, ship visits had reached 88 per season. In the same year, an estimated 1.8 million people visited Prince William Sound for recreation purposes. Much of the recreation and tourism in Prince William Sound and the Kenai Fjords National Park is related to the outstanding scenic beauty of the area and its pristine wilderness character. The Alaska National Interest Lands Conservation Act (ANILCA) created a 2.3-million acre wilderness study area in Prince William Sound.

The oil spill can be expected to affect tourism and recreation in the affected region of Alaska at least through the approaching summer season. The tourist industry already is reporting higher than normal cancellations on bookings for this summer. The magnitude and duration of these adverse consequences will depend in part on the speed and effectiveness of the cleanup and in part on the public's perception of its effectiveness in restoring the wildlife and scenic areas to their pre-spill condition. The spill is not expected to have a major detrimental impact on travel and tourism in the rest of Alaska.

Other Economic Effects

Native villages such as Tatitlek and Chenega on the shores of Prince William Sound depend on the animals, birds, fish, and plants of the sound and surrounding lands for their food. The existence of their traditional culture depends on the continuation of this subsistence economy. Losses or reductions in the availability of wild food sources cannot be measured adequately in dollars. Although the Natives are gaining some employment opportunities from Exxon's clean-up efforts, they remain deeply concerned about the long-term effects of the spill on their subsistence culture. There also is concern that beached oil and its cleanup may either destroy cultural resources or affect the ability of archaeologists to carbon date early sites. No single mechanism is in place at this time through which Alaska Natives can provide inputs on their particular concerns, or receive assistance for their claims and subsistence needs.

> There is no existing legislation that allows immediate aid to the local population affected by the spill.

Neither the oil spill nor its cleanup is expected to affect timber harvesting on national forest lands around Prince William Sound and on the Kenai Peninsula, and economic losses are unlikely. Some delay, however, in harvesting on Native Corporation and national forest lands on Montague Island may result from the spill. The U.S. Forest Service has had to extend the review period for the draft Environmental Impacts Statement because of oil spill response activities.

Early Lessons Learned/Recommendations

- The Department of the Interior, working with the State of Alaska and local Native leadership, should assist individual Alaska Natives and Native organizations in providing input into clean-up planning and filing claims for economic losses. This assistance should include the emergency provision of subsistence needs wherever required as a direct result of the spill.

- There is no existing legislation that allows immediate aid to the local population affected by the spill. In this incident, Exxon mitigated some of the economic losses to fishermen, Alaskan Natives, and other Alaskans through employment in the clean-up effort. Had there not been a responsible party who willingly assumed this financial burden, there would have been no immediate financial relief available to the affected population.

CHAPTER 2

Controversies Surrounding the *Exxon Valdez* Oil Spill

Exxon Reacted Responsibly to the *Exxon Valdez* Disaster

Frank Sprow, interviewed by Steve Curwood

In the following viewpoint, from an interview conducted ten years after the *Exxon Valdez* spill, Steve Curwood asks Frank Sprow about Exxon's responsibility and cleanup efforts. Sprow argues that Prince William Sound has recovered significantly, and that the sound is, as of 1999, a healthy biological community. Sprow concludes that, given its good faith efforts and the money it has already paid to compensate those affected, Exxon should not have to pay additional punitive damages. Steve Curwood is executive producer and host of the public radio show *Living on Earth*. Frank Sprow is the Exxon Corporation vice president for environment and safety.

Photo on previous page: A volunteer cleans the beach with paper towels and spoons. Critics questioned whether such cleanup efforts were useful, or even harmful. **(Natalie Fobes.)**

SOURCE. Steve Curwood and Frank Sprow, "Exxon Speaks," *Living on Earth*, March 5, 1999. © 2011 Living on Earth. Used with permission of *Living on Earth* and World Media Foundation. www.loe.org. *Living on Earth* is the weekly environmental news and information program distributed by Public Radio International. Use of material does not imply endorsement. Reproduced by permission.

Steve Curwood: . . . The Valdez oil spill's tenth anniversary is an occasion for deep reflection in Alaska, and it's revived bitter feelings that many have toward Exxon. Dr. Frank Sprow is Exxon's Vice President for Environment and Safety and joins us from Dallas, Texas. Tell me about March 24, 1989. Is that a date that haunts you folks at Exxon? I think in Alaska they use this phrase, "the day that the water died." How did you feel that your company was responsible for this?

Exxon's Responsibility

The Exxon Corporation hired local fishermen and paid them for the use of their boats and their time to help in the cleanup. (Time & Life Pictures/Getty Images.)

Frank Sprow: Well, I think you used a key word and that's "responsible." I heard about the spill on the radio, and when I got home and saw some of the video on television, I think it was a shocking sight. And when you realize that it was our oil and that we spilled it, that's a tough thing to stomach. You certainly knew that not only the

environment but people's lives were going to be strongly affected by this. And so I think if anything, you get a real resolve to do what you can to try to make it better.

Curwood: What do your experts say about when or if the region will be back to normal?

Sprow: By and large we see Prince William Sound as a healthy, robust, thriving biological community. The majority of species there are in good shape. Those that were affected by the spill. You can have acute, short-term effects, as we did in this spill. But the environment has remarkable powers of recovery, and rather straightforwardly and quickly re-establishes itself and the biological communities that are there.

Curwood: What about the Trustee Council and the National Oceanic and Atmospheric Administration [NOAA]? They have looked at this and they say that only 2 out of 11 key species, in their view, are fully recovered. How do you respond to those comments from the Trustee Council and NOAA?

Sprow: The problem, Steve, if you want to call it that, relates to the use of the phrase "recovery." The definition of recovery that some use is a return to 1989 conditions. Unfortunately, for most species, we don't know what their 1989 populations were. And perhaps even more importantly, the natural variability of changes in the Sound is such that you can't take a snapshot and expect at some future date for things to be as they were then. Our definition tends to be more in line with thinking biologically. Do we have a healthy biological system? Are the species that should be in the Sound there? Are they reproducing effectively? Do they have an adequate food supply? And on that measure we see the Sound as having essentially recovered.

Exxon Should Not Be Punished

Curwood: Let's talk about money for a moment. So far Exxon spent about 2-and-a-half billion dollars in cleanup

The Exxon Corporation

The Exxon Corporation grew out of another oil company giant, Standard Oil Company, founded by John D. Rockefeller (1839–1937) in 1870. . . .

In the 1860s Rockefeller foresaw the potential of refining Pennsylvania crude oil. Though internal combustion engines were not yet developed, kerosene oil could be used, among other things, to fuel lanterns. When Standard Oil was formed, it integrated all of the docks, railroad cars, warehouses, lumber resources, and other facilities it needed into its operations. Because of its size it was able to make lucrative deals with railroads. The result was to drive smaller refiners out of business. . . .

In 1882 Rockefeller and his associates established the first trust in the United States, which consolidated all of Standard Oil Company's assets in the states under the New York Company, in which Rockefeller was the major shareholder.

In the 1880s Standard Oil began producing as well as refining and distributing oil. It also began an overseas trade, particularly in kerosene to Great Britain. The trust encountered difficulties with the Sherman Antitrust Act of 1890, followed by an 1892 Ohio Supreme Court decision which forbade the trust to operate Standard of Ohio. The company then moved its base of operations to New Jersey, which in 1899 became home to Standard Oil of New Jersey, or Jersey Standard, the sole holding company for all of Standard's interests. Jersey Standard later became Exxon Corporation. In the first decades of the twentieth century Jersey Standard was banned from holdings in several states. Instead, it acquired companies in Latin America in the 1920s, particularly in Venezuela, and also expanded its marketing companies abroad.

As the supply of crude oil began shifting from the United States and

costs and another billion dollars with your out-of-court settlement with the state and Federal governments. You've also been ordered to pay another $5 billion in punitive damages to thousands of Alaskans, but your company is appealing this verdict. Can you tell me why, please?

Sprow: Before I do that, Steve, I might mention that there's one element of cost which you left out, and that's

Latin America to the Middle East in the 1920s, Jersey Standard and other companies effectively used the same monopolistic practices that John D. Rockefeller had used 50 years before to establish a foothold in the region. Middle East production was stepped up following World War II (1939–1945) and Standard Oil exploited its rich resources in Iraq, Iran, and Saudi Arabia. . . .

During the 1960s growing nationalism in the Middle East brought much resentment against the western companies dominating Middle Eastern oil. The Organization of Petroleum Exporting Countries (OPEC) was formed to protect the interests of the producing countries. As OPEC became more assertive, Jersey Standard sought other sources of crude oil. The company discovered oil fields in Alaska's Prudhoe Bay and in the North Sea. Around the same time, in 1972, Standard Oil of New Jersey officially changed its name to Exxon Corporation.

Financial difficulties beset the company in the 1970s, as the OPEC-induced oil shortage depleted much of Exxon's reserves. . . .

In 1989 the company was shaken by the *Exxon Valdez* disaster. . . . The state of Alaska conducted public hearings and Exxon was deemed to have been "reckless" by an Alaskan Grand Jury. Exxon lost a share of the world oil market to its competitor, Royal Dutch/ Shell in 1990. Still, teamed up with Pertamina, the Indonesian state oil company, Exxon in the 1990s developed the Natuna gas field. Exxon also agreed to a $15 billion development of three oil wells in Russia. A large oil discovery in 1996 in the Gulf of Mexico also allowed Exxon to court expansion plans far into the future.

SOURCE. *"Exxon Corporation,"* Gale Encyclopedia of US Economic History. *Detroit: Gale, 1999.*

the over $300 million which we immediately paid to those damaged by the spill. We worked with people to find out who was going to lose their fishing incomes, for example, and immediately paid those people for their loss of income, and in many cases also paid them for the use of their fishing boats and their own time and services to assist in the cleanup. So it was a lot of money paid to compensate for damages suffered in the spill. The

> The concept of punitive damages is just something we think is wholly inappropriate for this situation.

punitive damages that you mention we think are totally inappropriate.

Curwood: So, Exxon should not be punished for this.

Sprow: I think that what we have done is the responsible thing, in terms of the cleanup, the largest cleanup operation that's ever been taken on in the US. And the concept of punitive damages is just something that we think is wholly inappropriate for this situation.

Curwood: We've been hearing from people about the enduring lessons of the Valdez spill. And I'm wondering Dr. Sprow, if you'd just take a moment to tell us what you think is the lesson that has been learned by Exxon.

Sprow: That an ounce of prevention is worth a pound of cure. That's an old phrase, but if there were any disbelievers that that's a very accurate statement, they disappeared 10 years ago.

Curwood: I want to thank you for joining us. Dr. Frank Sprow is Vice President for Environment and Safety at the Exxon Corporation.

Sprow: Thanks very much for the opportunity to talk to you, Steve.

Exxon Acted Irresponsibly Following the *Exxon Valdez* Disaster

Susan Lyon and Daniel J. Weiss

In the following viewpoint from May 2010, the Center for American Progress argues that Exxon dodged responsibility after the spill. It notes that Exxon continued to make profits in the year of, and the years after, the spill and that Exxon fought paying compensation to those affected by the spill for two decades. Furthermore, they argue BP, which was responsible for some cleanup efforts, joined Exxon in trying to avoid responsibility and damages. In April 2010, a BP rig drilling for oil in deep water exploded, killing 11 people and gushing oil into the Gulf of Mexico. The oil flowed for three months before it could be stopped, causing serious damage to the Gulf environment. The authors note that BP was responsible for that major oil spill and should be forced to pay in full for that cleanup. Susan Lyon and Daniel J. Weiss are both environmental policy experts at the Center for American Progress.

ExxonMobil will convene its annual shareholders meeting in Dallas this morning as the magnitude of the ongoing BP oil disaster grows. This is a reminder that oil companies need to be held accountable for their actions—both while the oil gushes from the ocean floor and 20 years after the spill. The Exxon Valdez oil accident that slimed Prince William Sound in Alaska in 1989 is a chilling reminder of the need for government oversight and corporate accountability.

Exxon and BP's Broken Record

Many would assume that BP—the company responsible for the Gulf Coast disaster—will cover the entire cost of cleanup. But we learned from the Exxon Valdez spill that the reality is very different:

The Exxon Valdez tanker spilled more than 11 million gallons of crude oil into Alaska's Prince William Sound, which eventually contaminated approximately 1,300 miles of shoreline. The total costs of Exxon Valdez, including both cleanup and also "fines, penalties and claims settlements," ran as much as $7 billion. Cleanup of the affected region alone cost at least $2.5 billion, and much oil remains.

> An estimated 8,000 of the original Exxon Valdez plaintiffs have died since the spill while waiting for their compensation as Exxon fought them in court.

Yet Exxon made high profits even in the aftermath of the most expensive oil spill in history. They made $3.8 billion profit in 1989 and $5 billion in 1990. And this occurred while Exxon disputed cleanup costs nearly every step of the way.

Exxon fought paying damages and appealed court decisions multiple times, and they have still not paid in full. Years of fighting and court appeals on Exxon's part finally concluded with a U.S. Supreme Court decision in 2008 that found that Exxon only had to pay $507.5 million of the original 1994 court decree for $5 billion in punitive damages. And as of 2009, Exxon had paid only $383 million of this $507.5 million to those who sued, stalling on the rest and fighting the $500 million in interest owed to fishermen and other small businesses from more than 12 years of litigation.

Twenty years later, some of the original plaintiffs are no longer alive to receive, or continue fighting for, their damages. An estimated 8,000 of the original Exxon Valdez plaintiffs have died since the spill while waiting for their compensation as Exxon fought them in court.

Coastal regions and coastlines of the Prince William Sound are still contaminated. The Exxon Valdez Oil Spill Trustee Council's 2009 status report finds that as much as 16,000 gallons of oil remains in the sound's intertidal zones today. A 2001 National Oceanic and Atmospheric Administration study surveyed 96 sites along 8,000 miles of coastline and found that "a total area of approximately 20 acres of shoreline in Prince William Sound is still contaminated with oil. Oil was found at 58 percent of the 91 sites assessed and is estimated to have the linear equivalent of 5.8 km of contaminated shoreline."

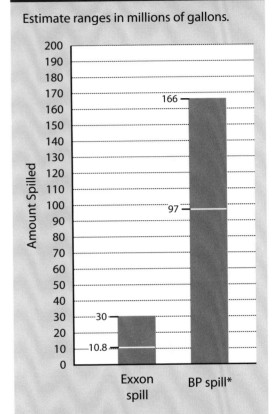

COMPARISON OF EXXON VALDEZ SPILL OF 1989 AND DEEPWATER HORIZON SPILL OF 2010

Estimate ranges in millions of gallons.

* This estimate is as of the end of June 2010. The Deepwater Horizon well continued to flow for another two weeks.

Taken from: Cindy Chang, "Alaska's Present, After 1989 Exxon Valdez Oil Spill, Might Be Gulf Coast's Future," Nola.com, June 27, 2010. www.nola.com.

Protesters in 2008 claimed that Exxon still had not paid the full amount of their fines assessed in the original 1994 court ruling against the company. (AFP/Getty Images.)

Animals and ecosystems suffered immediately after the spill and still do today. *Scientific American* reported that, "some 2,000 sea otters, 302 harbor seals and about 250,000 seabirds died in the days immediately following the spill." The researchers estimate that long term, "shoreline habitats such as mussel beds affected by the spill will take up to 30 years to recover fully."

Most of the oil cannot be mopped up. In fact, only about 8 percent was ever recovered. Dr. Jeffrey Short of Oceana testified at a hearing on the 20th anniversary of Exxon Valdez that, "Despite heroic efforts involving more than 11,000 people, 2 billion dollars, and aggressive application of the most advanced technology available, only about 8 percent of the oil was ever recovered. This recovery rate is fairly typical rate for a large oil spill. About 20 percent evaporated, 50 percent contaminated beaches, and the rest floated out to the North Pacific Ocean, where it formed tar balls that eventually stranded elsewhere or sank to the seafloor."

Exxon Fought the Courts, While BP Botched the Cleanup

Exxon didn't fail in its response efforts 20 years ago alone. BP actually joined Exxon in its response efforts—officially BP PLC, the same firm working to stop the gusher in the Gulf of Mexico now.

The Associated Press reports: "BP owned a controlling interest in the Alaska oil industry consortium that was required to write a cleanup plan and respond to the spill two decades ago . . . investigations that followed the Valdez disaster blamed both Exxon and Alyeska for a response that was bungled on many levels."

The same lack of preparation persists today, as BP workers and trained local employees and officials scramble to contain the gushing oil.

BP Profits While Disaster Unfolds

BP has made huge profits over the last 10 years. In fact, during the early days of the Gulf of Mexico disaster, BP was making "enough profit in four days to cover the cost of the spill cleanup" so far.

BP made $163 billion in profits from 2001 to 2009 and $5.6 billion in the first quarter of 2010. And *The Washington Post* found that, "BP said it spent $350 million in the first 20 days of the spill response, about $17.5 million a day. It has paid 295 of the 4,700 claims received, for a total of $3.5 million. By contrast, in the first quarter of the year, the London-based oil giant's profits averaged $93 million a day."

Meanwhile, contamination in the gulf continues to worsen. BP CEO Tony Hayward bet there would be a "very, very modest" environmental impact on the region, but the gulf's fisheries and shorelines will likely follow in the tragic path of the aftermath of the Exxon Valdez oil spill—ruined for decades after. Add thousands of gallons of chemical dispersants used for cleanup to this mix, along with their unknown but potentially toxic effects,

BP and the *Exxon Valdez*

Amy Goodman: What does the *Exxon Valdez* spill, Zyg Plater [environmental law professor at Boston College], have to do with BP?

Zygmunt Plater: It's so damnably frustrating to see this happening again, because BP dominated the Alyeska consortium . . . which was the entity that made all those decisions, but BP dominated Alyeska with a majority holding.

Amy Goodman: Explain, though, what Alyeska had to do with *Exxon Valdez*.

Zygmunt Plater: Well, the Trans-Alaska Pipeline System was organized by a consortium of seven companies, not one company. It was more like a partnership, and it ran everything, from the North Slope through the pipeline 800 miles down to Valdez to the tank loading areas and then the system of getting tankers down to California. It was a mega-system. . . . And BP was there in the beginning of *Exxon Valdez* by creating the preconditions that had hazards. . . . But the point was that this was not just a problem of an intoxicated captain, it was not just a problem of Exxon; it was through the mega-system. And the same problems we see in the Gulf [with the BP oil spill disaster] now, twenty years later, lessons unlearned.

SOURCE. Democracy Now, *"BP Played Central Role in Botched Containment of 1989* Exxon Valdez *Disaster,"* May 26, 2010, www.democracynow.org.

and this only compounds the damage to public health, tourism, and the region's greater economy.

NOAA has already shut down "nearly 20 percent of the commercial and recreational fisheries in the area because of the spill." And U.S. Commerce Secretary Gary Locke declared a fishery disaster in the Gulf of Mexico on Monday; the affected area includes Louisiana, Mississippi, and Alabama.

There is only more devastation to come to the communities in the region as their local populations and tourism industries suffer a blow not easily nursed back to health.

Holding BP Accountable for the Aftermath

BP cannot be let off the hook like Exxon was. No matter what anyone does, most of the gushing oil cannot be recovered; this is why BP must be responsible for regional restoration and cleanup—as well as plugging the hole.

BP needs to be held accountable for stopping the oil gusher and for shouldering the safety, health, restoration, and cleanup costs for years to come. President Obama created an independent commission to investigate causes and cleanup options for the disaster, and Congress is attempting to raise oil spill liability caps. But more steps need to be taken to hold BP fully accountable for the aftermath of the disaster.

BP should be required to place its 2010 first quarter profit of $5.6 billion in an escrow account to provide compensation to the fishermen, those in the tourist industry, and others whose livelihoods are threatened. These funds should also be used for cleaning up the soon to be blighted shores.

We are reminded as one of the largest environmental disasters in history continues to unfold in the gulf that we are putting our economy, national security, and environment at greater risk every day that the Senate fails to pass comprehensive clean energy and climate legislation. Yet ExxonMobil and BP both bragged that 2009 was a year of safety and environmental improvements for them; BP even claimed that, "2009 was an outstanding year" for their exploration and production efforts.

The BP Gulf Coast disaster reminds us that the offshore oil industry as a whole carries extreme risks that the American people cannot bear. We must act now to dramatically reduce our oil use, and President Obama and leaders in both parties of Congress must provide the leadership necessary to develop a clean energy and climate solution that becomes law this year.

Exxon's Damage Payments Should Be Limited

United States Supreme Court

The following viewpoint is an official summary of the 2008 decision by the Supreme Court of the United States that ended litigation against Exxon for the *Valdez* disaster. In the decision, the court concludes that the punitive damages designed to punish Exxon were too high at $5 billion. The court argues that very high punitive damages are unfair and unpredictable and thus fail to promote respect for the rule of law. The court concludes that to be consistent, under maritime law punitive damages should not exceed compensatory damages that directly repay those harmed by the disaster. Therefore, the court orders Exxon to pay $507.5 million dollars in punitive damages, the same amount as it paid total in compensatory damages. The Supreme Court opinion on this case was written by Justice David Souter.

SOURCE. *Syllabus of Exxon Shipping Co. et. al. v. Baker et. al.*, 2008. Copyright © 2008 Supreme Court of the United States. All rights reserved. Reproduced by permission.

In 1989, petitioners' (collectively, Exxon) supertanker grounded on a reef off Alaska, spilling millions of gallons of crude oil into Prince William Sound. The accident occurred after the tanker's captain, Joseph Hazelwood—who had a history of alcohol abuse and whose blood still had a high alcohol level 11 hours after the spill—inexplicably exited the bridge, leaving a tricky course correction to unlicensed subordinates. Exxon spent some $2.1 billion in cleanup efforts, pleaded guilty to criminal violations occasioning fines, settled a civil action by the United States and Alaska for at least $900 million, and paid another $303 million in voluntary payments to private parties. Other civil cases were consolidated into this one, brought against Exxon, Hazelwood, and others to recover economic losses suffered by respondents (hereinafter Baker), who depend on Prince William Sound for their livelihoods. At Phase I of the trial, the jury found Exxon and Hazelwood reckless (and thus potentially liable for punitive damages [a monetary award intended as a punishment]) under instructions providing that a corporation is responsible for the reckless acts of employees acting in a managerial capacity in the scope of their employment. In Phase II, the jury awarded $287 million in compensatory damage [a monetary award intended to repay for economic losses] to some of the plaintiffs; others had settled their compensatory claims for $22.6 million. In Phase III, the jury awarded $5,000 in punitive damages against Hazelwood and $5 billion against Exxon. The Ninth Circuit upheld the Phase I jury instruction on corporate liability and ultimately remitted the punitive damages award against Exxon to $2.5 billion.

Damages Were Excessive

Held:

1. Because the Court is equally divided on whether maritime law allows corporate liability for punitive damages

based on the acts of managerial agents, it leaves the Ninth Circuit's opinion undisturbed in this respect. . . .

2. The Clean Water Act's [CWA] water pollution penalties do not preempt punitive-damages awards in maritime spill cases. Section 1321(b) protects "navigable waters . . . , adjoining shorelines, . . . [and] natural resources," subject to a saving clause reserving "obligations . . . under any . . . law for damages to any . . . privately owned property resulting from [an oil] discharge." Exxon's admission that the CWA does not displace compensatory remedies for the consequences of water pollution, even those for economic harms, leaves the company with the untenable claim that the CWA somehow preempts punitive damages, but not compensatory damages, for economic loss. Nothing in the statute points to that result, and the Court has rejected similar attempts to sever remedies from their causes of action. . . . There is no clear indication of congressional intent to occupy the entire field of pollution remedies, nor is it likely that punitive damages for private harms will have any frustrating effect on the CWA's remedial scheme.

> The punitive damages award against Exxon . . . should be limited to an amount equal to compensatory damages.

3. The punitive damages award against Exxon was excessive as a matter of maritime common law [as established in earlier legal decisions]. In the circumstances of this case, the award should be limited to an amount equal to compensatory damages.

(a) Although legal codes from ancient times through the Middle Ages called for multiple damages for certain especially harmful acts, modern Anglo-American punitive damages have their roots in 18th-century English law and became widely accepted in American courts by the mid-19th century.

(b) The prevailing American rule limits punitive damages to cases of "enormity," in which a defendant's conduct is outrageous, owing to gross negligence, willful, wanton, and reckless indifference for others' rights, or even more deplorable behavior. The consensus today is that punitive damages are aimed at retribution and deterring harmful conduct.

(c) State regulation of punitive damages varies. A few States award them rarely, or not at all, and others permit them only when authorized by statute. Many States have imposed statutory limits on punitive awards, in the form of absolute monetary caps, a maximum ratio of punitive to compensatory damages, or, frequently, some combination of the two.

(d) American punitive damages have come under criticism in recent decades, but the most recent studies tend to undercut much of it. Although some studies show the dollar amounts of awards growing over time, even in real terms, most accounts show that the median ratio of punitive to compensatory awards remains less than 1:1. Nor do the data show a marked increase in the percentage of cases with punitive awards. The real problem is the stark unpredictability of punitive awards. Courts are concerned with fairness as consistency, and the available data suggest that the spread between high and low individual awards is unacceptable. The spread in state civil trials is great, and the outlier cases subject defendants to punitive damages that dwarf the corresponding compensatories. The distribution of judge-assessed awards is narrower, but still remarkable. These ranges might be acceptable if they resulted from efforts to reach a generally accepted optimal level of penalty and deterrence in cases involving a wide range of circumstances, but anecdotal evidence suggests that is not the case. . . .

Punitive Damages Should Be Fair

(e) This Court's response to outlier punitive damages awards has thus far been confined by claims that state-court awards violated due process. . . . In contrast, today's

Plaintiff's attorney Jeff Fisher makes a statement outside the Supreme Court. The court eventually ruled to cap punitive damages assessed against Exxon, declaring that fines should be predictable and consistent. (AP Images/ Lawrence Jackson.)

enquiry arises under federal maritime jurisdiction and requires review of a jury award at the level of judge-made federal common law that precedes and should obviate any application of the constitutional standard. In this context, the unpredictability of high punitive awards is in tension with their punitive function because of the implication of unfairness that an eccentrically high punitive verdict carries. A penalty should be reasonably predictable in its severity, so that even Holmes's "bad man" can look ahead with some ability to know what the stakes are in choosing one course of action or another.[1] And a penalty scheme ought to threaten defendants with a fair probability of suffering in like degree for like damage.

(f) The Court considers three approaches, one verbal and two quantitative, to arrive at a standard for assessing maritime punitive damages.

(i) The Court is skeptical that verbal formulations are the best insurance against unpredictable outlier punitive awards, in light of its experience with attempts to produce consistency in the analogous business of criminal sentencing.

(ii) Thus, the Court looks to quantified limits. The option of setting a hard-dollar punitive cap, however, is rejected because there is no "standard" tort or contract injury, making it difficult to settle upon a particular dollar figure as appropriate across the board; and because a judicially selected dollar cap would carry the serious drawback that the issue might not return to the docket before there was a need to revisit the figure selected.

(iii) The more promising alternative is to peg punitive awards to compensatory damages using a ratio or maximum multiple. This is the model in many States and in analogous federal statutes allowing multiple damages. The question is what ratio is most appropriate. An acceptable standard can be found in the studies showing the median ratio of punitive to compensatory awards. Those studies reflect the judgments of juries and judges in thousands of cases as to what punitive awards were appropriate in circumstances reflecting the most down to the least blameworthy conduct, from malice and avarice to recklessness to gross negligence. The data in question put the median ratio for the entire gamut at less than 1:1, meaning that the compensatory award exceeds the punitive award in most cases. In a well-functioning system, awards at or below the median would roughly express jurors' sense of reasonable penalties in cases like this one that have no earmarks of exceptional blameworthiness. Accordingly, the Court finds that a 1:1 ratio is a fair upper limit in such maritime cases.

(iv) Applying this standard to the present case, the Court takes for granted the District Court's calculation of the total relevant compensatory damages at $507.5 million. A punitive-to-compensatory ratio of 1:1 thus yields maximum punitive damages in that amount.

Note

1. Chief Justice Oliver Wendell Holmes argued in the early 1900s that law should be geared towards a hypothetical "bad man," who cared not about morality but only about avoiding punishment.

Exxon's Damage Payments Were Too Lenient

Eliav Bitan

The following viewpoint was written in 2008, just after the Supreme Court capped Exxon's punitive damages for the *Valdez* disaster. The author argues that this decision was wrong. He claims that Prince William Sound, the site of the spill, was seriously damaged, and that the sound has not recovered even 19 years after the disaster. In addition, he suggests that Exxon's profits are so high that the lower punitive damages administered by the court are not an effective punishment and will not deter the company from carelessness in the future. Eliav Bitan is an environmental activist.

This summer [2008], the Supreme Court released rulings on issues from the death penalty to gun control. One death that the Court failed to understand is the murder of Prince William Sound. This case began, of course, with the Exxon Valdez oil spill, the worst environmental disaster in American history. Thirteen hundred miles of shoreline were destroyed in 1989.

> The justices failed to adequately value the destruction of Prince William Sound.

The Supreme Court Failed

This event loomed over environmentalism in the 1990s as the prototypical example of petroleum gone wrong. Images of gulls, otters, and beaches covered in black lay like an oil slick on every video, magazine, or book that discussed environmental problems. The story of the Valdez spill ended this summer, and its final twists demonstrate that even though the environmental movement has built momentum and awareness, the Justices of the

Environmentalists argued that the fines assessed against Exxon failed to take into account the human costs suffered by the town of Cordova and other Alaskan communities. (**AP Images/ Al Grillo.**)

Supreme Court have not absorbed environmentalism's understanding of the value of an ecosystem. In the end, the justices failed to adequately value the destruction of Prince William Sound.

The court ruled correctly on the first issue of the case—was Exxon responsible for the spill? Exxon suggested the only fault was with Capt. Joseph Hazelwood, the drunken Valdez captain who'd left the bridge at the critical moment leading to the spill. The legal question is whether Exxon should be held liable for the actions of an employee who was violating company policy by drinking on duty. The court found that Exxon knew the captain was an alcoholic, and their decision to allow him to continue in his position meant they had to take responsibility for his actions.

Having resolved the question of whether Exxon bears legal responsibility for the spill, the Court turned to the issue of financial reparation. Exxon has already spent millions on direct remuneration for damages, and billions on clean up from the spill. This money, used for direct damages, was held to be appropriately spent.

The second sum of money Exxon contested, the far larger sum, was punitive damages. Punitive damages are intended to deter an agent from committing the crime in the future. According to Slate, Exxon argued that because they "did nothing malicious, nothing intentional, and that 'the company didn't stand to make $1 profit' from the spill, that they had already suffered enough."

Exxon claimed that because the spill was an accident, and not an intentional action intended to make money, they had no incentive to repeat the incident. Exxon, according to their lawyers, didn't need to be scared away from further spills, because they would avoid them on their own.

In response to this, those injured by the spill pointed out that Exxon's placement of an alcoholic captain at the helm constituted misconduct. Exxon had increased prof-

Justice Stephen Breyer Dissents

I disagree with [the Court's] conclusion . . . that the punitive damages award in this case must be reduced. . . .

In my view, a limited exception to the Court's 1:1 ratio is warranted here. "As the facts set forth in Part I of the Court's opinion make clear, this was no mine-run case of reckless behavior. The jury could reasonably have believed that Exxon knowingly allowed a relapsed alcoholic repeatedly to pilot a vessel filled with millions of gallons of oil through waters that provided the livelihood for the many plaintiffs in this case. Given that conduct, it was only a matter of time before a crash and spill like this occurred. And as Justice [Ruth Bader] Ginsburg points out, the damage easily could have been much worse.

The jury thought that the facts here justified punitive damages of $5 billion. . . . The District Court agreed. It "engaged in an exacting review" of that award "not once or twice, but three times, with a more penetrating inquiry each time," the case having twice been remanded for reconsideration in light of Supreme Court due process cases that the District Court had not previously had a chance to consider. And each time it concluded "that a $5 billion award was justified by the facts of this case," based in large part on the fact that "Exxon's conduct was highly reprehensible," and it reduced the award (slightly) only when the Court of Appeals specifically demanded that it do so.

When the Court of Appeals finally took matters into its own hands, it concluded that the facts justified an award of $2.5 billion. . . . It specifically noted the "egregious" nature of Exxon's conduct. And, apparently for that reason, it believed that the facts of the case "justifie[d] a considerably higher ratio" than the 1:1 ratio we had applied in our most recent due process case and that the Court adopts here.

I can find no reasoned basis to disagree with the Court of Appeals' conclusion that this is a special case, justifying an exception from strict application of the majority's numerical rule. The punitive damages award before us already represents a 50 percent reduction from the amount that the District Court strongly believed was appropriate. I would uphold it.

SOURCE. *Opinion of Breyer, J.* Exxon Shipping Co. et al v. Baker et al, *554 U.S. 07-219 (2008).*

its by not spending sufficiently on maintaining the safety of their operations. Punitive damages would ensure that Exxon alter their business practices to avoid future spills.

Calculating Punitive Damages

How much should those punitive damages be? The original jury that heard the case ruled it ought to be $5 billion, and a higher court reduced the punitive damages to $2.5 billion. How much is $2.5 billion for Exxon? The plaintiffs calculated that Exxon makes $2.5 billion in profits every three weeks.

> What Justice Souter didn't list was the destruction to human life caused by the spill.

How much has Exxon paid already? $507 million to compensate the 32,000 native Alaskans, averages about $15,000 in compensation per person. Exxon has spent $3.4 billion on fines and clean-up. About 4 weeks of profit.

So how did the majority of the Court find in this case? Justice [David] Souter, writing for the 5 judges of the majority, presented a gripping description of the actions of the captain and his crew that led to the crash. The justice narrates events closely, telling how many drinks the captain had (5 double vodkas), and what his blood alcohol content was (.241). Justice Souter recounted where Hazelwood stood, when he went below decks, who was left at the bridge.

When the decision proceeds to describing the events after the spill, we lose the heart-wrenching detail. Justice Souter lists numbers. He lists the numbers of the laws that Exxon broke, and he lists the costs of the clean-up. What Justice Souter didn't list was the destruction to human life caused by the spill.

What was destroyed by the Valdez spill? The Prince William Sound, which was home to not only a vibrant marine ecosystem but also a precious human community as well. . . . With no roads in or out, the people of

Cordova, in Prince William Sound, could leave the keys in their cars' ignitions. But what was lost here is not just another rural village, but, also a vital part of our nation's food system. As they say, "The world is hungry and we feed them good food—the best. And that's really precious too." Instead of salmon, they have nothing but "Beaches and bays full of more oil than you can imagine." . . .

Instead of mentioning the destruction of this place, Justice Souter's learned opinion gave a remarkable history of punitive damages stretching back to the code of Hammurabi, and including the creation of the American Constitution, and Anglo-American precedents and common law. He reviewed various American states' legal policies on punitive damages, as well as various nations' policies on punitive damages. He notes that many states and nations do not offer this opportunity for retribution and deterrence. Justice Souter expressed the Court's disgust and disagreement at the vast differences in punitive awards granted by different juries when considering cases which share basic facts. The court, he says, would like to eliminate unpredictable punitive awards by instituting more rigorous standards.

What should that standard be? Justice Souter, and the majority, settled on a one-to-one ration between damages and punishment. As Exxon had paid $507 million dollars in compensation, they should pay no more than $507 million dollars in punitive damages.

There is no adequate justification given for why punitive damages should bear a specific relation with compensatory damages. Justice Souter even points out that "punitive damages are designed to punish and deter, they ought to take into account the defendants' financial condition and the magnitude of harm caused."

The defendants' financial condition is flush, and the harm caused here massive. In his dissent, Justice [John Paul] Stevens wrote that "In light of Exxon's decision to permit a lapsed alcoholic to command a supertanker carrying tens of millions of gallons of crude oil through the treacherous waters of Prince William Sound, thereby endangering all of the individuals who depended upon the sound for their livelihoods, the jury could easily have given expression to its moral condemnation of Exxon's conduct in the form of this award."

A Win for Business

For the final analysis of this decision, let's turn simply to *Forbes* magazine. A journal explicitly of wealth, the magazine gives us an unfettered analysis from the point of view of big business. The title of the article is: "Exxon Ruling Big Win for Business." The article reads in part:

> ExxonMobil officials couldn't immediately be reached for comment. It's certainly a bittersweet victory—$507.5 million is a hefty sum for anyone—but consider what might have been had the justices let stand the lower court's $2.5 billion penalty award. What ExxonMobil must now pay also pales in comparison to the company's record first-quarter profits of $10.9 billion on $116.8 billion in revenues.

Is this ruling enough to punish and deter Exxon? Does this ruling adequately compensate the people and ecosystems whose lives have been irrevocably altered by the spill? I'm afraid not.

Exxon Needed to Do More Cleanup Following the *Exxon Valdez* Spill

Mauricio Roman

The following viewpoint was written in the MIT paper a few months after the *Exxon Valdez* disaster. The author argues that Exxon should not have ceased its cleanup efforts at the end of the spring following the disaster. He says that most of the oil released by the tanker has not been recovered, and that if the oil is not cleaned up it will continue to damage the environment for decades. He notes that Exxon was unprepared to deal with the spill, and that as a result a full cleanup is impossible. He concludes that Exxon's efforts were halfhearted and inadequate and urges the government to force Exxon to do more. Mauricio Roman was a student at MIT at the time of the spill.

Last week Exxon stopped indefinitely its cleanup efforts on its March 24 [1989] Alaskan oil spill, leaving behind thousands of dead birds and sea otters, shattered ecosystems, hundreds of miles of beaches covered with tar, and thousands of unemployed fishermen. Exxon only managed to clean up a fraction of the spill it created, leaving nature to repair the damage and the public to pay for the consequences. The question Exxon is forgetting about is: will nature repair the damage, and if so how long will it take?

Most of the Oil Remains

A recent report says Exxon only cleaned up 2.5 million gallons out of the 11 million spilled, mostly with the paid help of fishermen and their boats. According to another report, hundreds of miles of coastline fouled by the spill still remain uncleaned and those that were treated were inadequately cleaned.

> Exxon decided to clean up its image instead of its spill and pull out indefinitely as soon as summer was over.

Exxon promised to clean up every barrel of oil spilled. However, as it faced the reality that it was almost completely unprepared to do so in the first few days after the spill—when it would have been much easier to collect the oil—and that as time went by the cost of an effective cleanup soared, Exxon decided to clean up its image instead of its spill and pull out indefinitely as soon as summer was over.

As is widely known, Exxon lacked organization and equipment when the oil spill occurred. A reconstruction study published in the *New York Times* shows that much of the 11 million gallons of oil spilled on Alaska's shorelines could have been contained in the first hours of the accident. According to the study, the first full emergency crew from Alyeska Pipeline Service Company, a subsidiary of Exxon and other oil companies with interests in

Alaska, did not arrive at the spill for 14 hours and the crippled tanker was not surrounded by floating oil containment booms for another 21 hours. By the time full emergency action was taken, the oil was out of any effective control, the study says.

Exxon claims that if it had been allowed by the Coast Guard to apply chemical dispersants the magnitude of the spill would have been significantly smaller. In fact, this method breaks up the oil but does not eliminate it; instead, it hides it underwater. According to scientific studies done on previous oil spills, the dispersed oil descends in the water column and in large quantities can be dangerous to fish and other marine creatures.

The oil spill rapidly extended southward. After seven days it extended ninety miles, and after two months oil could be found as far as 470 miles away. By July it was estimated that 730 miles of beach were contaminated with oil. The Wilderness Society makes the observation that if the *Exxon Valdez* had gone aground off Cape Cod, oil would be fouling most of New Jersey's shoreline and all the beaches of Cape May, Delaware, and Maryland as well as the northern Outer Banks of North Carolina—all this after devastating most of the Eastern Seaboard between Boston and New York City, including Long Island Sound.

As the deadly blanket of oil spreads southward, the public saw on its TV screens workers in orange suits wiping rocks with cloths and blasting out oil with hoses. Exxon's beach effort, however, was limited to the same 1500 yard stretch of beach for the first six weeks, according to a report released by the Wilderness Society. At the same time, Exxon was sending a pamphlet to millions of credit card holders saying that "by mid-May, essentially all of the oil on the water had been removed or had been dissipated."

It was not until May 2 that Exxon released a plan to clean the coastline affected by the spill. The plan stated

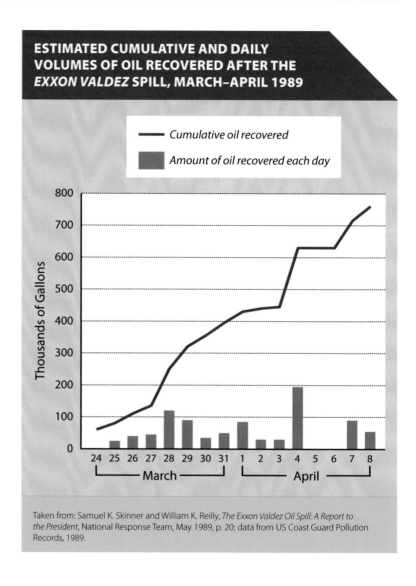

ESTIMATED CUMULATIVE AND DAILY VOLUMES OF OIL RECOVERED AFTER THE *EXXON VALDEZ* SPILL, MARCH–APRIL 1989

— Cumulative oil recovered

■ Amount of oil recovered each day

Taken from: Samuel K. Skinner and William K. Reilly, *The Exxon Valdez Oil Spill: A Report to the President*, National Response Team, May 1989, p. 20; data from US Coast Guard Pollution Records, 1989.

that only 364 miles of coastline would be "treated" and made no provisions for continuing cleanup beyond mid-September. It also said that 191 miles of lightly-oiled coastline would not be cleaned at all.

By accepting this plan, the Coast Guard, which supervised the cleanup since two weeks after the spill, not only signed off 200 miles of coastline but allowed Exxon to clean up the coastline according to its own standards.

Superficial Cleaning Efforts

Exxon's treatment of beaches consisted of washing the oil ashore with high-pressure hoses and wiping it off rocks with absorbent pads. Exxon's claim, echoed by publications such as *Newsweek*, is that they have done their best and it is nature's turn to repair the damage. Some scientists and government officials disagree; they have reasons to believe that Exxon's beach treatment is superficial, and that fragile ecosystems might have been radically affected for many years to come. Some of the reasons they give are:

- Oil becomes embedded in the fine-grained sediment in the intertidal zone and shallow bottom areas when washed ashore. Wave and tidal action and storms then cause the sediment to act like a time-release capsule—emitting clouds of oil into the water periodically over months, years, even decades, to continuously infect the microorganisms on which fish and other marine life depend. Marine ecologist Robert Howarth estimated in *Science* magazine that this effect will last for more than 20 years. To reduce this effect, treatment of oil-affected coastline should include shoveling the sand and sediment in order to remove the oil that has penetrated the surface, according to the Wilderness Society report.

> " The Bush Administration's decision to leave the cleanup to Exxon instead of federalizing the spill response was a colossal blunder. "

- Exxon's coastal cleanup was concentrated on beaches exposed to wind and storms, which help remove the oil, rather than in coves and inlets where the oil is likely to remain much longer.

- Beaches were treated only once; many of these will be blanketed again with the oil remaining in the water.

- While studies of oil spills in tropical waters have shown that certain bacteria help decompose the oil, the gelid temperatures on the Gulf of Alaska will most probably slow down the bacterial effect.

The long term effects of the spill are unknown, but will most certainly be worse than that of any other spill in this country, especially when there are still 8.5 million gallons of slowly decomposing oil in Prince William Sound and its surrounding coastline. To ignore the potential destructive power of the remaining oil on the ecologic system is to turn the back on the future of Alaska's ecology and economy. So far, ruined fishing seasons and death tolls show the effect on the ecosystem: 33,000 birds and 980 sea otters are known to have died.

In retrospect, the [President George H.W.] Bush Administration's decision to leave the cleanup to Exxon instead of federalizing the spill response was a colossal blunder. However, if Exxon promised to "leave Prince William Sound the way we found it," as Don Cornett, Exxon's public-affairs manager, said just after the spill, then it should either do so or admit its failure, but not launch a campaign of disinformation. Six months after the spill, it is virtually impossible to retrieve every drop of oil from the ocean or wipe clean every rock on the coastline. However, with a net income of $5.26 billion, Exxon can do a much better job than it has done so far. The federal government, with the help of Congress and the state of Alaska, should ensure that Exxon complies with its promises by pressuring it to continue the spill cleanup next spring in a more thorough and organized manner than it did this summer.

Photo on previous page: Secretary of the Interior Manuel Lujan (holding hose) helps clean up oil in Naked Island, Alaska. Critics maintained that such cleanup efforts were geared more toward rehabilitating Exxon's public image than toward restoring the ecosystem. (AP Images/ Rob Stapleton.)

Exxon's Cleanup Efforts Had Mixed Effects on Local Communities

Joanne B. Mulcahy

The following viewpoint, published 12 years after the spill, explains that native communities on the Alaskan island of Kodiak were destabilized by the influx of money from Exxon for cleanup efforts. The communities were also hurt when the oil damaged fisheries. As a result, alcoholism, drug abuse, and depression all increased. However, the author also notes that the disaster had some long-term benefits. Exxon's payments helped fund building projects, and the disaster created a heightened sense of community among native populations. Joanne B. Mulcahy is a writer and ethnographer.

O n March 24, 1989, the *Exxon Valdez* rammed a reef in Prince William Sound, dumping 10.8 million gallons of crude oil. Despite the dis-

---

SOURCE. Joanne B. Mulcahy, *Birth and Rebirth on an Alaskan Island: The Life of an Alutiiq Healer*. Copyright 2001 by Joanne B. Mulcahy. Reprinted by permission of the University of Georgia Press.

tance, currents carried oil hundreds of miles southwest, affecting nearly one thousand miles of coastal water around Kodiak [an island in Alaska]. The date was Good Friday, a significant marker for Kodiak Natives. On a Good Friday twenty-five years before, many of the same communities were hit by the largest earthquake in North America during modern times. The event had multiple repercussions, negative and positive. Some villages were physically destroyed, which forced residents to relocate, but new skills and technologies also came with community recovery. The earthquake and tsunami that followed remain pivotal in the minds and life stories of Kodiak's Native people, particularly their dual legacy of displacement and adaptability.

> "The men 'treated' the oily beaches . . . for the unheard-of wages of $16.69 per hour. Berries went unpicked, fish unharvested, families unattended as Akhiok residents worked round the clock."

Money and Drink

The *Exxon Valdez* oil spill didn't hit Kodiak area beaches until mid-April, but the salmon season was ruined for the year, which disrupted the normal cycle of subsistence. In Akhiok [a village on Kodiak Island], villagers stayed sober through most of the summer as they assisted in the cleanup effort. The men "treated" the oily beaches—the word "cleanup" had been banned by Exxon officials—for the unheard-of wages of $16.69 per hour. Berries went unpicked, fish unharvested, families unattended as Akhiok residents worked round the clock. At first, no one worried when someone cracked a beer after a long day's work. It was not until fall, when Exxon sent out the last of the salary checks, that the most toxic fallout spread. Into the villages, cash flowed with the same rich abundance that the thick oil spread across the seals and ptarmigan and sea life. Like those of an aftershock, the results proved as disastrous.

People in the village began to drink openly. Exhaustive news coverage followed. Tribal Council President Dave Eluska Sr. . . . tried to stress the village's strengths over its frailties. Eluska pointed to the ongoing cultural revitalization as a foundation for recovery. In September, a response team composed of religious leaders, KANA [Kodiak Area Native Association] employees, and RuralCap officials, flew to Akhiok to initiate a "healing process." They facilitated "healing circles" to talk about grief, spirituality, and recovery, a melding of the AA model, Russian/Native religious traditions, and cultural revitalization.

The Kodiak Alutiiq Dancers perform at a convention of Alaskan natives. Many in the Alutiiq Nation felt a greater sense of community after the *Exxon Valdez* oil spill. (John Wagner/ZUMA Press/Corbis.)

Long-Term Effects

The long-term effects of the oil spill would prove most significant. In studies later conducted by anthropologists, Akhiok's reaction was mirrored elsewhere. In interviews with 594 men and women in thirteen communities, researchers found diminished social relations, declines in subsistence practices and in health status, increases in drinking, drug abuse, and domestic violence, and increased post-traumatic stress and depression, especially in women. However, there were also long-term positive effects, including compensatory funding from Exxon. Some funds were directed to publications such as an entire issue of *Arctic Anthropology*, others to building projects, one of which became the Alutiiq Museum and Archaeological Repository.

Further, [cultural anthropologist and Alaska native] Nancy Yaw Davis points to community survival strategies that were tested and strengthened by the oil spill. She writes, "The residents in very small communities seem to have a philosophy of tolerance, a resiliency to disruptions, a sense of humor, and a traditional fisherman's perspective that if things are bad this year, they will probably be better next year. . . . Also, village residents have family—they are rich in relatives." Another result was a heightened sense of community and unified ethnicity among Alutiiq [a Native Alaskan ethnicity] people. A chief from one village noted that "now we know more about our relatives in Prince William Sound." A series of regional elders' conferences further enhanced this sense of connection. All these shifts would ultimately strengthen the village of Akhiok.

Oil Cleanup Has Been Improved as a Result of the *Exxon Valdez* Spill

Jessica Marshall

The following viewpoint reports that the response to the Deepwater Horizon oil spill of 2010 in the Gulf of Mexico has been influenced by lessons learned from the *Exxon Valdez* spill. Because of the *Valdez*, cleanup workers and scientists were better prepared with equipment to deal with the Gulf disaster, the author says. The *Valdez* spill also taught scientists that many cleanup efforts, such as washing beaches with hot water or cleaning birds with soap, actually do more harm than good. She also notes that the *Valdez* taught scientists that oil stays in the environment far longer than people used to think, so preventing it from reaching beaches in the first place is a high priority. Jessica Marshall is a science writer for *Discovery*.

Ａs 42,000 gallons of crude oil a day erupt from the sea floor in the Gulf of Mexico at the site where an oil rig caught fire and sank [in 2010], responders are working against the clock to contain and redirect the oil to keep it from hitting shore. But the degree to which this spill will be able to be cleaned up remains to be seen, according to experts.

The Gulf Spill vs. the *Valdez* Spill

One potentially helpful fact is that because the leak is around 50 miles offshore, teams have greater ability to protect the coastline than in the infamous 1989 spill in Prince William Sound, Alaska, when the oil tanker *Exxon Valdez* ran aground and dumped nearly 11 million gallons of crude oil along the coastline and killed tens of thousands of birds and other wildlife.

> Lessons learned and legislation passed following the *Valdez* spill will be guiding the efforts to contain the oil now spewing into the Gulf.

"No two oil spills are the same," said Stanley Rice of the National Oceanic and Atmospheric Administration in Juneau, Alaska, who has studied the aftermath of the *Valdez* spill for the last 20 years.

Nonetheless, lessons learned and legislation passed following the *Valdez* spill will be guiding the efforts to contain the oil now spewing into the Gulf.

"I think one lesson over time is, to have the equipment and be ready for the spill," Rice said. "The other lesson is, once it gets into sediments or wetlands it's very difficult to deal with. There's going to be a lot of effort to keep it from getting to wetland shores."

"I think we're in really strong shape," said oil spill scientist Chris Reddy of the Woods Hole Oceanographic Institution in Woods Hole, Mass. As a result of the Oil Pollution Act of 1990, passed following the *Valdez* spill, stakeholders carry out practice drills in anticipation of

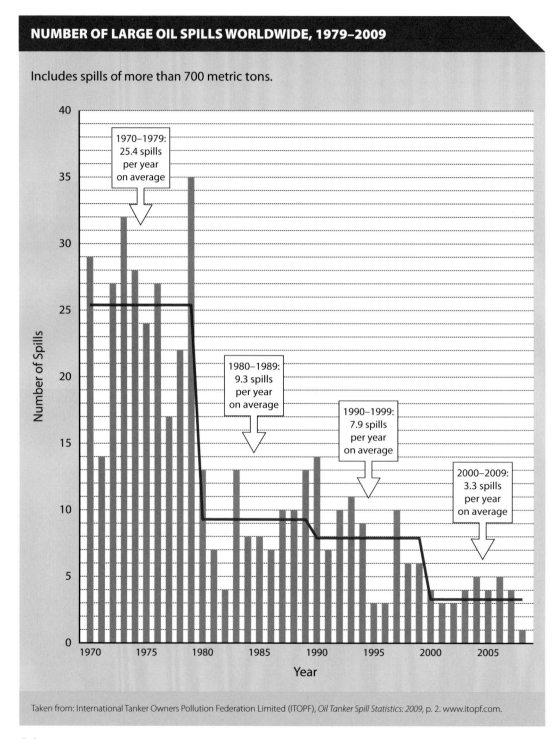

NUMBER OF LARGE OIL SPILLS WORLDWIDE, 1979–2009

Includes spills of more than 700 metric tons.

1970–1979:
25.4 spills
per year
on average

1980–1989:
9.3 spills
per year
on average

1990–1999:
7.9 spills
per year
on average

2000–2009:
3.3 spills
per year
on average

Number of Spills

Year

Taken from: International Tanker Owners Pollution Federation Limited (ITOPF), *Oil Tanker Spill Statistics: 2009*, p. 2. www.itopf.com.

spills and have a coordinated procedure for responding. "Were in really good hands," he said.

But he agrees every spill requires a tailored response that can't entirely be anticipated. "We have very little knowledge of deep water spills," he said, in contrast with a tanker spill where the oil is released at the surface. "You have the plume of oil coming upward. How it behaves at the surface depends on the type of oil, the currents, the water temperature."

Crude oil is a complex mixture of chemicals. Evaporation will remove some of the oil components, including many of the most toxic compounds, Reddy explained.

Other crude oil components will dissolve into the water. This helps by diluting these chemicals into a larger volume—the entire water column instead of just the surface—but these compounds are often toxic and until they can be widely dispersed, they may reach concentrations high enough to kill ocean life.

> One of the lessons of the *Valdez* is that the effects of a spill can persist far longer than researchers anticipated.

Over time, other processes will play a role. "Nature's bacteria do a tremendously good job of cleaning up oil spills," Reddy said, by eating the oil for energy. "But there's usually some lag time before the bacteria kick in."

Booms, Bouts, and Dispersants

Meanwhile, human efforts at the beginning include setting out booms that surround the oil to keep it from spreading. Oil skimming boats can suck up the contained oil, and snares that look like cheerleaders' pom poms can be set out on the spill to soak up oil and then be removed.

Dispersants can be used to break the oil into droplets that can dissolve into the water. Although they remove oil from the surface where it threatens birds and mammals,

Booms such as this one in Prince William Sound were designed to keep oil from reaching the shore. (Time & Life Pictures/Getty Images.)

their downside is that they bring the oil into the water where animals like fish and shrimp can be exposed.

The goal, Rice said, is to protect places where long-term contamination is likely: "The lesser of two evils is not to have the habitat affected," he said. "We're willing to absorb more acute mortalities in the short term. If the habitat gets contaminated we have this chronic situation where several species are affected over long periods of time."

Indeed, one of the lessons of the *Valdez* is that the effects of a spill can persist far longer than researchers anticipated. "We used to think of things in terms of a couple of years, Rice said. "Now we think of things in a couple of decades."

For instance, a recent study in *Environmental Toxicology and Chemistry* showed that harlequin ducks in Prince William Sound are still exposed to oil. These birds live in shallow water near the shore and eat mussels and snails, which makes them especially vulnerable to continued exposure to oil trapped in beach sands, said study lead author Daniel Esler of Simon Fraser University in Burnaby, British Columbia.

"Most of the residual oil and especially the stuff that's still potentially toxic to wildlife is buried in the sediment of the beaches," Esler said. "If you were there right after a storm or if an otter had just been there digging, the oil would still be liquid and still have an odor to it."

"The amount of oil that is there is a teeny fraction of what spilled," he added. "But a teeny fraction of 11 million gallons is still a lot of oil."

Salt marshes along the Gulf Coast, like the shallow shore areas of Prince William Sound, provide sediments and lots of little pockets where oil can be trapped and stay. "If it does make it to the beaches and the marshes, the lesson from the *Exxon Valdez* is that it's likely to be there for a while and it's not going to be good for wildlife," Esler said.

Another lesson from the *Valdez* is that certain approaches do more harm than good. Steam cleaning rocks on beaches after the *Valdez* spill killed barnacles and mussels, says ecologist Dee Boersma of the University of Washington in Seattle. She adds that many of the birds people tried to save by washing with soap to remove the oil died anyway—with only the added stress of the washing and human handling to show for it.

"Washing sand or rocks or birds doesn't do a lot of good," Boersma told Discovery News. "It just makes us feel better."

Oil Cleanup Has Not Been Improved as a Result of the *Exxon Valdez* Spill

Eric Nalder

In the following viewpoint, a reporter argues that since the *Exxon Valdez* spill, there has not been any major improvement in oil spill response. He says that despite legislation, oil spill readiness remains insufficient, and there is not enough equipment available to deal with serious spills. Further, he says, there have been few improvements in cleanup technology, which still relies on booms, skimmers, and techniques much like those that were available for the *Valdez* spill. As a result, he concludes, oil spill cleanup after the Deepwater Horizon of 2010 is inadequate. Eric Nalder is an investigative reporter who won a Pulitzer Prize for his coverage of the *Exxon Valdez* disaster in the *Seattle Times*.

SOURCE. Eric Nalder, "Exxon Valdez: What Did We Learn?" *Houston Chronicle*, May 16, 2010. Copyright © 2010 by Houston Chronicle. Reproduced by permission.

Tons of *Exxon Valdez* oil still afflicts the beaches of Prince William Sound, just under the surface—more persistent than the lessons learned from a disaster that killed 250,000 seabirds and 3,000 sea otters.

The magnitude and danger unraveled in the hours, days—even years—afterward as oil spread across the water with winds, current and tide.

Still Unprepared

And yet, two decades after 10,000 workers, 1,000 boats and 100 aircraft labored without major success to mop up the spill in Alaska, the weapons available for today's [2010] fight in the Gulf of Mexico remain virtually the same.[1]

That, despite lawmakers' vows that it would never happen again.

Crude oil from the misdirected Exxon tanker killed wildlife, sickened cleanup workers and absorbed $2 billion in cleanup monies, and it doesn't even rate among the top 30 spills worldwide.

Congress passed the Oil Pollution Act of 1990 even before the Prince William Sound cleanup was declared over.

It mandated among other things a multiagency federal effort to research better ways to clean up oil spills.

Yet the taxpayer money dedicated to new cleanup tools after 1989 was never adequate. The research task may have been too tall. Since 1990, the agency that spent the most on "oil spill research"—the Interior Department's Minerals Management Service [MMS]—has doled out a tenth of a penny for every dollar it collected in royalties from oil companies for their offshore drilling rights, according to a *Houston Chronicle* analysis of agency budget documents.

MMS kept its oil spill research budget at roughly $6 million a year for two decades—for a total of $129 million—while royalties came in during the same period totaling $107 billion, records show. U.S. Coast Guard spending dwindled from $7 million in 1992 to just $600,000 last year.

Two other agencies, the EPA [Environmental Protection Agency] and the National Oceanic and Atmospheric Administration [NOAA], spent less, according to congressional reports. Overall federal spending fell far below a planned $28 million a year, and the multiagency task force filed its last research plan 13 years ago.

> Without advancements in technology, hope must rest on . . . a 'backwoods' list of cleanup approaches . . . and patience while nature absorbs the stain.

MMS spokesman Nicholas Pardi said in an e-mail that two thirds of the agency's money supports a 667-foot-long New Jersey wave pool which is "fully booked" for testing cleanup equipment.

Technology Has Not Advanced

Without advancements in technology, hope must rest on what California Congresswoman Lynn Woolsey dubs a "backwoods" list of cleanup approaches: Skimmers and barges, booms, igniters for burning, dispersants, biological agents, a variety of beach scrubbing methods and patience while nature absorbs the stain.

"The basic tool kit hasn't changed dramatically, or at all," said Jeff Short, a former NOAA scientist now with the environmental group Oceana.

Craig Rassinier of Houston led the initial attack on the *Exxon Valdez* spill and is soberly watching BP officials tackle a massive leak from the uncontrolled oil well off the Louisiana coast. The former Exxon official, like other experts, understands the considerable limitations of the 38 skimmers, including a dozen oceangoing vessels, assigned to the Gulf spill.

"Once it gets out of the bottle, you are not putting it back in, and you are playing chase," he said. "I can plan

Skimmers used to clean up the oil spilled from the Deepwater Horizon in 2010 in the Gulf of Mexico were not a significant improvement over the technology available during the *Exxon Valdez* oil spill in 1989. **(Getty Images.)**

for a certain point, I just can't go beyond that. No matter what I want to do, I can't get there."

Nearly every spill cleanup expert and veteran interviewed for this story volunteered or ultimately admitted a persistent caveat. It is the other lesson learned from *Exxon Valdez*, besides the one that says preventing oil spills is the only sure course.

It is that sopping up enough oil to satisfy public expectations is impossible once more than a million gallons are in the water. Success is collecting more than 10 or 20 percent of the goo, studies show. Half is unheard of.

Frank Larossi, the Houston-based president of Exxon shipping back in 1989, had little to offer to BP: "I don't have any advice to give them," said the retired maritime executive widely criticized during the *Exxon Valdez* cleanup. "I don't think there's a solution."

BP itself painted a nightmare scenario in a cleanup plan updated last year for federal regulators. Required to describe a "worst case discharge," BP imagined a blowout near the Deepwater Horizon spewing 50 times more oil each day.

"Is a bigger one of some sort coming?" asked Rex Redfern, of Tomball, who retired in January 2003 as Conoco's program director for spill preparedness and response. "It's when, not if. It's probably going to be a tanker spill."

Last year [2009], legislation to increase federal spending on better oil cleanup research and to reorganize the effort died in the U.S. House of Representative's Science and Technology Committee—the victim of other priorities.

"The energy behind it just floated away, shame on me and shame on us," said Woolsey, the California Democrat who co-sponsored the bill after a slow response to a relatively small spill in San Francisco Bay in 2007. "I didn't push."

> Complacency about cleanup capacities undermined readiness in the Gulf of Mexico as it did in Alaska before *Exxon Valdez*.

The law she tried to amend, OPA 90, did have some positive outcomes.

Cleanup equipment is more abundant because the law forced all major oil handlers to place under contract a certain capacity of cleanup resources. That inspired a manufacturing boom. But the law didn't mandate newer techniques or better skimmers and boom, just more of them with more capacity.

Complacency Undermined Readiness

Among those concerned is Dan Lawn, a former Alaska environmental regulator, who remembers the optimism that infected industry executives prior to and during the first days of the *Exxon Valdez* spill, and the derision he faced when he questioned it.

At 3 A.M. on March 24, 1989, Lawn became the first state government official to board the *Exxon Valdez*, stepping over a mound of oil onto a rope ladder, from a harbor pilot boat floating on two feet of crude. He recalls a powerful odor like being "imbedded in a gas tank" and how awkward it was greeting Capt. Joe Hazelwood on the bridge.

Retired from the Alaska Department of Environmental Conservation, Lawn believes complacency about cleanup capacities undermined readiness in the Gulf of Mexico as it did in Alaska before *Exxon Valdez*. He cited flaws in the system set up by OPA 90 to determine how much equipment oil handlers must have ready for a spill.

Companies like BP must contract for certain amounts of equipment that can arrive in time to fight a spill. But federal standards require a theoretical capacity, not proven ability to perform.

West Coast states, particularly Alaska, passed tougher laws requiring more equipment with better performance standards. Today there are 108 skimmers and nearly 50 miles of boom in Valdez Harbor, making it one of the best-equipped harbors in the world.

By contrast, fewer skimmers and less boom capacity were on the pre-spill inventories for a total of 14 locations covering the Gulf of Mexico from Texas to Florida. That's according to websites for BP's two primary contractors, Marine Spill Response Corporation and the National Response Corporation.

When cleanup started, only seven big offshore skimmers were available in the Gulf, so five were imported from the East Coast, said Coast Guard Capt. Ed Stanton, incident commander for the Louisiana Coast. BP's preparedness plan was approved last year by federal regulators, but crews still needed more boom, he said.

Since *Exxon Valdez*, skimmers have seen incremental improvements in scooping volume and maintenance. Newer Norwegian booms move faster through the water before losing effectiveness and can withstand higher waves. But the basic physics remains the same.

Luck has favored the Gulf cleanup. The Southern Louisiana crude oil is less viscous than the thicker Alaskan crude oil, evaporating more quickly and dispersing more easily. The shorelines of the Gulf are farther from the spill source than was the *Exxon Valdez*.

Burning and dispersants were used early in the Gulf of Mexico, and dispersants are being applied to the underwater source of the spill, presumably to greater effect.

BP's burning of oil on the water is a tricky process by which crude must be concentrated behind fireproof booms before it is ignited.

Both techniques—burning and dispersants—were easier to employ in the Gulf than in Prince William Sound because they have become less controversial. But wind and waves have halted skimming for half of the cleanup days, and there have been only 13 burns, Stanton said.

Could researchers someday provide better tools? Redfern, the former Conoco executive, said he doesn't know.

"We let the market develop new technologies for us, and none came up," he said. "That still doesn't change the fact the current technology is not very good."

Note

1. In April 2010, the oil rig Deepwater Horizon exploded in the Gulf of Mexico. The well gushed oil into the gulf for months.

Canada Has Failed to Implement Effective Drug Testing Despite the *Exxon Valdez* Disaster

Jeff Gray

The following viewpoint reports that the *Exxon Valdez* disaster, which was caused in part by the captain's intoxication, led to a push for random drug and alcohol testing in jobs involving public safety in North America. Such laws were generally accepted in the United States. In Canada, however, they are still contested twenty years after the disaster, the author says. He explains that in Canadian law, random alcohol and drug testing is often seen as violating a worker's rights, but that companies are likely to continue to push for testing because the cost of *Valdez*-like disasters is so high. Jeff Gray is a reporter on business and other issues for the *Globe and Mail*, a newspaper based in Toronto.

Both the BP oil spill in the Gulf of Mexico and the rupture of the *Exxon Valdez* oil tanker off the coast of Alaska in 1989 left oil-soaked birds, ruined shorelines and economic woes in their wake.

Safety vs. Workers' Rights

But the *Valdez* accident also had a wider impact on employment law in North America. According to witnesses in the court battles after the Alaska disaster, the captain of the *Valdez* had downed five double vodkas at waterfront bars before taking the helm. This accounts for the Alaskan catastrophe's other legacy: A push by oil companies and other industries to test employees in dangerous jobs for drugs and alcohol.

Two decades later, this push is still working its way through Canada's complex ecosystem of labour boards, human rights tribunals and courts—and somewhat unevenly, legal experts say. Courts, labour arbitrators and rights adjudicators in Alberta have been more open to drug and alcohol testing than those in other parts of Canada.

Some say a Supreme Court of Canada ruling is needed to settle the question. Meanwhile, the cases keep popping up. One of the latest pits unionized workers against the Irving Pulp and Paper Mill in Saint John. This month, the New Brunswick Court of Queen's Bench heard arguments from the company, which wants to overturn an arbitrator's ruling that struck down a policy of random alcohol testing.

"This goes back in earnest—and the timing is interesting—to the *Exxon Valdez* crisis. That's when companies like Exxon and in Canada, Imperial Oil [a unit of Exxon], said, 'We can't take any chances any more,'" said Richard Charney, the head of Ogilvy Renault LLP's employment-law practice, who has fought a number of drug-and-alcohol testing cases on behalf of corporate clients.

Canadian Human Rights Commission Alcohol and Drug Testing Policy

The following types of testing are *not acceptable*:

- Pre-employment drug testing

- Pre-employment alcohol testing

- Random drug testing

- Random alcohol testing of employees in non-safety-sensitive positions.

The following types of testing *may be included* in a workplace drug- and alcohol-testing program, but only if an employer can demonstrate that they are *bona fide* [authentic] occupational requirements:

- Random alcohol testing of employees in safety-sensitive positions. Alcohol testing has been found to be a reasonable requirement because alcohol testing can indicate actual impairment of ability to perform or fulfill the essential duties or requirements of the job. Random drug testing is prohibited because, given its technical limitations, drug testing can only detect the presence of drugs and not if or when an employee may have been impaired by drug use.

- Drug or alcohol testing for "reasonable cause" or "post-accident," e.g. where there are reasonable grounds to believe there is an underlying problem of substance abuse or where an accident has occurred due to impairment from drugs or alcohol, provided that testing is a part of a broader program of medical assessment, monitoring and support.

- Periodic or random testing following disclosure of a current drug or alcohol dependency or abuse problem may be acceptable if tailored to individual circumstances and as part of a broader program of monitoring and support. . . .

- Mandatory disclosure of present or past drug or alcohol dependency or abuse may be permissible for employees holding safety-sensitive positions, within certain limits, and in concert with accommodation measures. Generally, employees not in safety-sensitive positions should not be required to disclose past alcohol or drug problems.

SOURCE. *Canadian Human Rights Commission Policy on Alcohol and Drug Testing, Executive Summary, June 2002. www.chrc-ccdp.ca/pdf/poldrgalceng.pdf.*

"So the motivation is actually one of workplace safety and public safety."

The idea has been widely accepted in the United States for workers in safety-sensitive jobs, so the push from U.S. oil companies in Alberta is not surprising. But in Canada, companies that have brought in drug- or alcohol-testing policies have run into arguments at labour and human rights tribunals that alcohol or drug addiction is a disability, and thus testing employees—and disciplining those who are impaired on the job—is a form of discrimination.

Alcohol Test vs. Drug Tests

Canadian courts have also distinguished between the more complex business of testing for illegal drugs, such as marijuana or cocaine, and the established and reliable Breathalyzer-type test for alcohol, which can immediately show if a worker is impaired. Drug tests, often involving urine analysis, take several days to show results and do not necessarily demonstrate that the employee was impaired while working.

> The most-invasive testing policies . . . remain difficult to defend in Canada.

New technology may overcome this hurdle, but so far it has not. Last year, the Ontario Court of Appeal upheld an arbitration board's decision to strike down Imperial Oil's random drug-testing policy at its refinery in Nanticoke, Ont., even though the company was using a new saliva-testing method it argued could determine with more precision whether an employee was impaired on the job.

Some testing, such as in cases when an employer has "reasonable cause" to suspect a worker in a safety-sensitive job is impaired, is generally allowed in Canada. Workers can also be tested as part of a package of conditions for returning to work after being caught for drug or alcohol abuse, Mr. Charney said.

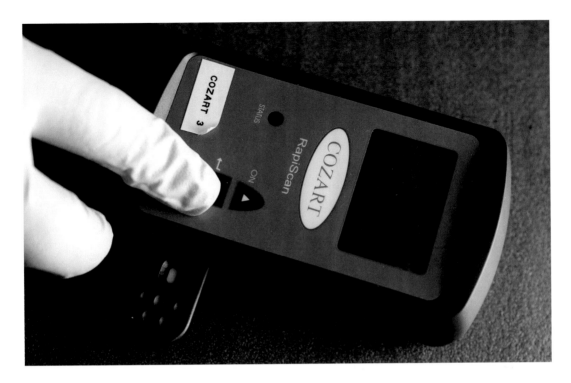

Saliva-testing methods used by the Imperial Oil company to detect drug use were struck down by Canadian courts even though the company claimed the tests could determine precisely if an employee is impaired while on the job. (Getty Images.)

Lawyers who act for employers point to a key case, known as John Chiasson v. Kellogg, Brown & Root (Canada) Co., as ammunition in their fight to expand the scope of employee testing. In that case, the Alberta Court of Appeal upheld the right of employers to administer drug tests to applicants for safety-sensitive posts even before they are hired, and to choose not to take on casual marijuana users. (The Supreme Court of Canada declined to hear an appeal of that ruling in 2008.)

While Alberta regulatory bodies have been more receptive to the push for employee oversight, the most-invasive testing policies—those that demand random drug and alcohol tests of all workers in safety-sensitive posts—remain difficult to defend in Canada.

For alcohol, it may be allowed in certain circumstances, Mr. Charney said. For drugs, it can be put in place if the employer can prove that an "out of control" drug culture exists among its workers.

That factor accounts for the different attitude of Alberta's courts, human rights adjudicators and labour arbitrators, said Barbara Johnston, head of Stikeman Elliott LLP's employment law group in Calgary and a veteran of high-profile testing cases.

She cites the well-documented drug and alcohol problems found in Fort McMurray, Alta., and other northern Alberta oil-boom communities, where numbers of largely young, male, well-paid oil workers are thrown together, often without family or other social support.

"When you look at the context of what's happening in Alberta, I think the cases make very clear sense," said Ms. Johnston, who represented major oil companies, including Syncrude Canada Ltd. and Imperial Oil Ltd., that intervened in the Chiasson case.

Dan Scott, of Seveny Scott Lawyers in Edmonton, who has acted for labour unions, says he believes big oil companies will continue to bring in new testing policies, even if they could face sanctions from human-rights tribunals. The reason, he suggests, is simple: The penalties they face for violating an employee's human rights pale in comparison with the millions of dollars in fines or cleanup costs after a major accident.

Prince William Sound Is Recovering from the Oil Spill

National Oceanic and Atmospheric Administration

In the following viewpoint, the federal agency of the United States government focused on the condition of the oceans and the atmosphere argues that, as of 2005, most of the oil from the *Exxon Valdez* is no longer in the environment of Prince William Sound. They report that the ecosystem in Prince William Sound is stabilizing, though scientists still monitor the sound to determine whether the oil spill continues to stress the environment. They conclude that, while Prince William Sound will not return to its exact condition before the spill, the area, along with its plant and animal populations, appears to be recovering.

SOURCE. National Oceanic and Atmospheric Administration, "Prince William's Oily Mess: A Tale of Recovery," March 3, 2005 (Revised March 25, 2008). http://oceanservice.noaa.gov.

*W*hat was the ultimate fate of the 10.8 million gallons of oil released from the Exxon Valdez? Nobody knows for sure, but based on the areas that were studied in the aftermath of the spill, scientists made estimates of the ultimate fate of the oil. A 1992 National Oceanic and Atmospheric Administration (NOAA) study provided some insight, estimating that the great majority of the oil photolysed [chemically decomposed by exposure to light] in the atmosphere, dispersed into the water column or degraded naturally (biodegraded by microorganisms or photolysed in the water). Cleanup crews recovered about 14 percent of the oil, and approximately 13 percent sank to the sea floor. About 2 percent (some 216,000 gallons) remained on the beaches.

> Considering that nearly 11 million gallons escaped from the tanker, and that large quantities eventually fouled shorelines in the sound and elsewhere, very little remains.

Little Oil Remains

Considering that nearly 11 million gallons escaped from the tanker, and that large quantities eventually fouled shorelines in the sound and elsewhere, very little remains. . . .

At the sites being studied by scientists, surface oil had all but disappeared by 1992, three years after the spill. The apparent increase in surface oiling in 1991 (two years after the spill) was likely to have been caused by heavy equipment digging up buried oil (called "berm relocation"), which was used as a remedial technique that year.

However, oily traces of the spill can still be found on some beaches. The remaining oil generally lies below the surface of the beaches in places that are very sheltered from the actions of wind and waves (which help to break down and remove stranded oil), and on beaches where oil initially penetrated very deeply and was not removed.

At these beaches, there are signs of weathered oil on the surface and deposits of fresher oil buried beneath. Sometimes this oil makes its way to the surface and can be seen as a sheen on the water as the tide comes in. Interestingly, despite the fresh appearance of oil at these sites, chemical analysis and biological observations indicate that the oil is actually of such low toxicity that many intertidal organisms can tolerate its presence, even though it can accumulate in their tissues.

One of the scientists' goals is to determine whether this residual oil is causing environmental harm to organisms living there, since one of the most difficult questions to answer during any oil spill is, "How clean is clean?" That is, when does cleanup begin to cause more harm than simply leaving the oil in place to degrade naturally?

In addition, reports both in the news and in scientific journals have stated that not all of the oil found in Prince William Sound can be traced back to the *Exxon Valdez*. This is not surprising. Many potential alternate sources of hydrocarbons exist in the marine environment, even in a region that is relatively unpolluted. As examples:

- Some of the hydrocarbons are natural, coming from undersea oil seeps or forest fires.
- Others are definitely of human origin, such as the rupturing of oil storage tanks during the Alaskan earthquake of 1964, the pumping of ship ballast tanks, and fuel leakage from commercial ships and recreational boats traveling through the area.

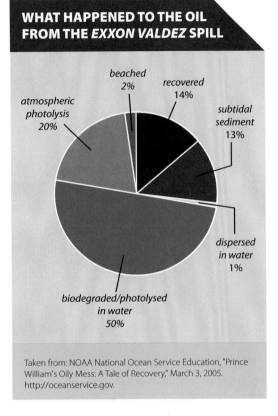

WHAT HAPPENED TO THE OIL FROM THE *EXXON VALDEZ* SPILL

beached 2%
recovered 14%
subtidal sediment 13%
atmospheric photolysis 20%
dispersed in water 1%
biodegraded/photolysed in water 50%

Taken from: NOAA National Ocean Service Education, "Prince William's Oily Mess: A Tale of Recovery," March 3, 2005. http://oceanservice.gov.

Chemists who "fingerprinted" hydrocarbon residues in both beach sediments and in animal tissues found that not all of the oil came from the *Exxon Valdez*. More recently, the highest concentrations of oil in mussel tissues have come from small boat harbors and diesel fuel. However, scientists hypothesize that most of the oil contamination found in Prince William Sound does trace back to the *Exxon Valdez*. . . .

An Ecosystem in Transition

One of the most abundant alga on the shorelines of Prince William Sound [is] *Fucus gardneri*, commonly called "rockweed" or "popweed." Because this algae favors the middle part of the intertidal zone, where much of the heavy oiling and cleanup occurred, its abundance declined in many areas of the Sound. Beginning in 1990, scientists saw the cover of rockweed increase steadily at oiled sites—until 1994, that is. From 1994 through 1995, there appeared to be a noticeable decline in cover, especially at sites that had been oiled.

What caused the decline in 1994 and 1995?

Scientists don't know for certain. Here are some possibilities:

- It is possible that the oiling or cleanup (or both) in 1989 killed the original stands of rockweed, so that the normal mix of plants of different ages was not present. Instead, the areas became dominated by plants of all the same age because they were reestablished all at the same time after the spill. In 1994, all these plants would have reached the end of their life cycle at the same time, leading to the decrease evident in the graph. The die-off of plants of all the same age would not be noticeable under normal circumstances because plants of all different ages would be present.

- Alternatively, an explosion in the population of grazers (such as periwinkle snails) that feed on algae two

Photo on previous pages: *Fucus gardneri*, or rockweed, in Prince William Sound recovered quickly beginning in 1990 before declining noticeably in 1994. (Gerald & Buff Corsi/Visuals Unlimited/ Corbis.)

and three years after the spill may have had something to do with the decline in rockweed.

- Perhaps it is a subtle, longer-term toxic effect of oiling. Or, it might have nothing at all to do with the spill or cleanup. Data collected in the coming years will help shed light on these conditions.

What do these trends over time mean for recovery in Prince William Sound?

Scientists think they suggest that highs and lows in abundance of plants and animals will continue as the system adjusts itself. With time, natural controls will dampen the fluctuations in abundance of marine life. Most of these adjustments will not be noticeable, and to the casual observer, conditions will continue to look much as expected in an area that remains a very beautiful place to visit. However, these subtle changes may have implications for how scientists view the process of recovery from the one-time stress of an oil spill. Eventually, the changes also may affect other parts of the ecosystem that are commercially and aesthetically important, such as the fisheries and tourist destinations. NOAA scientists will continue to study the sound until 2005 in an effort to answer these questions. . . .

Has Prince William Sound recovered?

We all have some idea of just what "recovery" is— we've all recovered from a cold or the flu—yet to ecologists studying natural systems, it is a very difficult term to define and measure. If you ask a fisherman from Kodiak Island, a villager from the town of Valdez, an Exxon engineer—or, yes, a NOAA biologist—you are likely to receive such different answers that you may wonder if they heard the same question!

An ecosystem like Prince William Sound constantly adjusts itself to react to, or compensate for, changes in the environment, such as:

- daily temperature variations;
- changing of the seasons;
- long-term drought;
- rare natural events, like hurricanes and earthquakes; and
- oil spills.

When the *Exxon Valdez* spill occurred in March 1989, the Prince William Sound ecosystem was also responding to at least three notable events in its past:

- an unusually cold winter in 1988–89;
- growing populations of reintroduced sea otters; and
- a 1964 earthquake.

Scientists studying the effects of the spill must evaluate their results against this background of other insults, or stressors, that have affected the sound.

Scientists do not define recovery as a return to the precise conditions that existed before the oil spill. They know that this is unlikely to happen. Nevertheless, they can observe a range of conditions to measure shoreline recovery from the spill.

> Biologists consider the intertidal communities in Prince William Sound to be still recovering, but not completely recovered.

For example, if they find that unoiled sites are changing in the same ways and at similar rates as the oiled sites, then the changes are probably caused by natural events and cannot be linked to the oil spill. If conditions at oiled sites fall outside the range found at control sites, then scientists would suspect that oil contamination is still affecting these systems.

Just as people differ in their ability to recover from injury, so do plants and animals. Some animals and plants are resilient and grow back quickly. In Prince William Sound, green algae and certain types of worms grew back the first summer. Rockweed and barnacles had repopulated many areas within 2 to 3 years. Other animals, such as clams, limpets, and some snails, are taking much longer.

In short, biologists consider the intertidal communities in Prince William Sound to be still recovering, but not completely recovered.

Scientists will continue to regularly monitor a range of study sites in Prince William Sound at least through the year 2005. In 2001, they began a smaller-scale, experimental phase of their research, focusing on fewer sites. Scientists will use this information to improve oil spill response and cleanup in the future, with an overall goal of minimizing environmental harm. Because of this, the *Exxon Valdez* will leave at least one positive legacy in its unfortunate wake: knowledge that will benefit all of us and the environment the next time disaster strikes.

Serious Effects of the Oil Spill Linger Twenty Years Later

Exxon Valdez Oil Spill Trustee Council

The *Exxon Valdez* Oil Spill Trustee Council includes state and federal trustees and was formed to oversee restoration of Prince William Sound through the use of the $900 million civil settlement. In the following viewpoint, the trustee council argues that toxic oil remains in the environment of the sound twenty years after the spill. The council notes that to varying degrees, otters, killer whales, and other species continue to suffer ill effects, both because of the disruption of the initial spill and because of the stress caused by oil still in the environment. The continuing environmental problems also affect humans who are economically dependent on the sound.

Visitors today experience the spectacular scenery and wildlife of Prince William Sound and the North Gulf of Alaska. However, one of the most

SOURCE. *Exxon Valdez* Oil Spill Trustee Council, "2009 Status Report." Courtesy of the *Exxon Valdez* Oil Spill Trustee Council.

stunning revelations of Trustee Council-funded monitoring over the last ten years is that *Exxon Valdez* oil persists in the environment and, in places, is nearly as toxic as it was the first few weeks after the spill.

Continuing Toxicity

This was not expected at the time of the spill or even ten years later. In 1999, beaches in the Sound appeared clean on the surface. Some subsurface oil had been reported in a few places, but it was expected to decrease over time and most importantly, to have lost its toxicity due to weathering. A few species were not recovering at the expected rate in some areas, but continuing exposure to oil was not suspected as the primary cause.

In 2001, researchers at the Auke Bay Laboratories, NOAA Fisheries, conducted a survey of the mid-to-upper intertidal in areas of Prince William Sound that

Most of the killer whales that died as a result of the *Exxon Valdez* oil spill died immediately rather than from prolonged exposure over time. (AP Images/John Gaps III.)

William Sound have recovered, local populations in heavily-oiled areas have not recovered as quickly.

Sea otters excavate pits while foraging for food, including their preferred food item, clams. Sometimes these pits are excavated in the intertidal zone. Using depth recording instruments, researchers have looked at the data from more than 10 million dives. These data have shown that sea otter diving activities within the intertidal zone are centered around the zero tide elevation up to +1–2 feet above that. Although they have a fur coat, sea otters lack the thick, insulating layer of blubber found in other marine mammals. Thus, they rely on a high caloric intake to maintain their body temperature. To do this, otters must consume about 25% of their body weight each day. This requires each otter to dig thousands of pits each year.

> Where clam beds and lingering oil patches overlap, it is likely that digging pits continues to expose sea otters to oil.

Sea otters usually have very small home ranges, typically consisting of a few square kilometers. In these small ranges, it is unlikely the otters are avoiding areas of lingering oil when foraging. Unfortunately, where clam beds and lingering oil patches overlap, it is likely that digging pits continues to expose sea otters to oil. The otters digging activities do reduce the amount of subsurface oil in the long term: in the process of digging a pit, sediments and the subsurface oil are released and re-suspended in the water and exposed to weathering.

Current Trustee Council-funded studies monitor environmental damage from the remaining oil. Additional studies have been funded to determine where in the spill-affected area subsurface oil may persist, and what, if anything, to do about it.

Following the oil and its impacts over the past 20 years has changed our understanding of the long-term damage from an oil spill. Because of the scope and duration of the restoration program, lingering oil and its effects were discovered and tracked. As a result, we know that risk assessment for future spills must consider what the total damages will be over a longer period of time, rather than only the acute damages in the days and weeks following a spill. Beaches in the Gulf of Alaska are unique because of their composition and structure and the lack of waves and winter storm action. This, along with the colder temperatures, is partly why oil has persisted and remained toxic here. The potential for long-term damage remains wherever oil persists after an oil spill, whether it is buried in the ocean bottom, marshes, mangroves, or in other non-dynamic habitats.

> " The losses to killer whale populations resulted primarily from the initial, acute exposures to the spill. "

In addition to the continued impacts of lingering oil discussed above, several species have not demonstrated full recovery from the initial damage caused by the spill. The status of killer whales is a clear example of these long-term effects.

Case Study: Killer Whales

Killer whales are individually identifiable and fortunately in Prince William Sound they were photographed starting in 1984, five years prior to the spill. Thus, researchers knew the numbers and associations of the whales at the time of the spill. Two groups of killer whales were photographed in slicks of oil in the weeks following the spill. These two groups lost approximately 40% of their numbers by 1990, and an additional five whales after 1990. One of these, the AB pod, is a "resident" fish-eating group of killer whales, and does show some signs of recovery. The second group is a small, unique population known as "AT1." They are "transient" killer whales that feed on marine mammals. They show no signs of recovery and continue to decline.

The losses to killer whale populations resulted primarily from the initial, acute exposures to the spill. Most carcasses were not found following the spill—which was not surprising since killer whale carcasses are known to sink—but the missing individuals have never been seen or photographed again. It is thought that the damage to killer whales from the spill, like many of the mortalities of other marine mammals, was caused by the inhalation of the oil's toxic fumes, as all of these species had to breath air from a few inches above the slick.

Whale pods are integral, matrilineal families. So a spill that kills any of the key members of the pod, especially reproductive-age or older females, can have far reaching consequences. The reproductive capacity of the pod was reduced by the loss of females which even under ideal conditions have a low reproductive rate, with only about half of newborn calves surviving. Since pods are matrilineal, the loss of these females means that the leaders of the pod are also lost. Some of the females that disappeared following the spill also had young offspring that died in the first few years after the spill, likely due to the loss of their mothers. In addition, the AB pod has shown signs of an unusual social breakdown within the group, with one matrilineal group leaving to join a different pod. This is a phenomenon not seen in any other resident pod in the North Pacific.

> The Prince William Sound ecosystem is incredibly complex and the interactions between a changing environment and the injured resources and services are only beginning to be understood.

Resident killer whales in Alaska have generally been increasing since the 1980s. However, the recovery of the AB pod is slower than the growth of other fish-eating pods in Prince William Sound or in Southeast Alaska. Their full recovery to pre-spill levels will likely take an additional decade or more, if their recovery is not further compromised. For the transient

AT1 population, there appears to be no hope for recovery. There has not been a successful recruitment to the pod since prior to the spill. This unique population will likely become extinct as the remaining members continue to age and die.

Status of Injured Resources and Services

In November 1994, the Trustee Council adopted an official list of resources and services injured by the spill as part of its Restoration Plan. When the Restoration Plan was first drafted, the distinction between the effects of the spill and the effects of other natural or human-caused stressors on injured natural resources or services was not clearly delineated. The spill was recent, the impact to the spill-area ecosystem was profound, and adverse effects of the oil on biological resources were readily apparent. As time passes, however, the ability to distinguish the effects of the oil from other factors affecting fish and wildlife populations becomes more difficult.

Through hundreds of studies conducted over the past 20 years, we have come to understand that the Prince William Sound ecosystem is incredibly complex and the interactions between a changing environment and the injured resources and services are only beginning to be understood. For example, seabirds will have difficulty recovering without the recovery of herring, which is a vital food source; species in the intertidal zone will continue to be compromised until we can determine the amount and distribution of lingering oil; and human services cannot be recovered until rockfish, herring, and cutthroat trout are recovered. These complexities, and the difficulties in measuring continuing impacts from the spill, mean that determinations about the status of a resource or service contain some inherent uncertainty.

Now, 20 years after the spill, there are two species that continue to be listed as "not recovered," ten species and four services listed as "recovering" (including Barrow's goldeneyes, added to the list in 2008 based on their continuing exposure to oil), five listed as "unknown," and ten listed as "recovered."

Herring were affected in 1989 by the spill, and the herring numbers in Prince William Sound are still too low to sustain a commercial fishery. The 1989 year class had the lowest recruitment ever measured. However, that alone does not explain the present low populations of Prince William Sound herring. Their population crash was detected in 1993, some three years after the spill. In addition, herring populations historically fluctuate and can be affected by a myriad of factors. Due to these factors, there continues to be debate as to when the decline started and whether it was directly linked to the spill.

While the cause of the continued decline in Prince William Sound herring populations remains uncertain, it is certain that the Sound cannot be considered recovered until healthy herring populations have returned. Herring harvests had always been a vital resource for human communities in the Sound prior to the spill. Herring also provide crucial biological links between species within the ecosystem. Forage fish, such as herring, connect the production of algae and zooplankton to large predators such as other fish, birds and marine mammals. The recovery of some seabird populations is likely affected by the depressed herring population. Herring, rich in natural oils, contain significant amounts of energy. The oceanic ecosystem and its inhabitants rely on such energy transfers, and herring, even with the depressed numbers of today, are likely to play a critical role in energy transfer to other species.

Herring recovery is a current focus of Trustee Council studies. The vital role herring play for both human and marine animal communities is clear, but the path to restoring this important species is uncertain. Herring populations are driven by complicated forces, including disease, predation, and oceanographic dynamics. Any proposed restoration for this species will require a careful understanding of these complex dynamics.

CHAPTER 3

Personal Narratives

Friends of Prince William Sound Remember Its Past and Contemplate Its Future

Debra McKinney

In the following viewpoint written in the weeks after the spill, an *Anchorage Daily News* reporter discusses her own experiences of interacting with nature and wildlife in Prince William Sound before the disaster. She says that the damage to the sound is like losing a friend, and says that she and many others are grieving following the spill. McKinney interviews a state park director, a fisherman, and residents who live and work in the sound. All talk about encounters with wildlife like bears, orcas, and otters, and express fear that the sound will be environmentally and economically damaged, perhaps permanently.

Photo on previous page: Cordova District Fishermen United president Jerry McCune sits through a 1989 meeting of local fishermen discussing their bleak future. (**AP Images/John Gaps.**)

SOURCE. Debra McKinney, "A Friend Is Sick," *Anchorage Daily News*, 1989. Copyright © 1989 Anchorage Daily News (adn.com). All rights reserved. Reproduced by permission.

I've tried to write about friends who died, as if casting memories in print might hold the emptiness back a little longer. But I could never get beyond a few sleepless nights of worry over where to begin. So I'd let it go, write sympathy cards and decide what kinds of trees to plant in their honor once the ground thawed in spring.

Grieving for Prince William Sound

I feel the same way about Prince William Sound, although this is a friend I refuse to bury. The Sound isn't dead, but it's very, very sick. My heart is sick, too.

For those who have never spent much time on the Sound, it would be like coming home to find your house ransacked and obscenities spray painted all over the walls. Or having someone you love lapse into a coma, and not knowing if he'll ever be the same again. Or having your church burn to the ground.

I've always wanted to spend a whole summer in the Sound, to watch seals and otters raise their pups, and visit the secret beach where orcas come to rub their bellies. I wanted to spend time in Derickson Bay, described by a friend as "Yosemite being born." Its glacier carved granite walls, the El Capitans [a rock formation in Yosemite National Park] of the Sound, rise from below the ice to meet the clouds. Twice I've tried to get there. Twice weather chased me away.

I decided I'd go to the Arctic National Wildlife Refuge instead this summer. There might be oil drilling up there someday, and I want to see the refuge before it's too late. Prince William Sound, I figured, would always be there.

Parts of the Sound are still pristine. Cold, strong winds blowing off glaciers in Blackstone Bay and the fjords of Port Wells may be able to push away wandering fingers of oil should they come calling. Meanwhile, oil is reaching into the mouth of one of my most cherished places, Port Nellie Juan.

My friend Louisa Rand introduced me to that corner of the Sound. She spent her first summer in Alaska there, working on a shrimp boat. She tells of a brilliant day of feasting on the bounty of the ocean seafood caught that day and a loaf of bread she baked in the galley oven. The sky was the most elegant shade of blue. Life was all around.

It Will Never Be the Same

"We were in heaven," she recalled recently. "I really could have died out there and it wouldn't have mattered."

Kayaking with Louisa through Culross Passage to Port Nellie Juan was slow going. She had to take it all in—every bird, every ripple in the ocean, every movement in the trees. Have you ever seen such water, she asked. So pure.

Beyond the Sound, oil is starting to leave an industrial ring around Kenai Fjords National Park. On a kayak trip there, in Aialik Bay, we counted black bears on two hands and saw so many seals and pups hauled out on ice floes we couldn't begin to count them.

At one point, we stopped paddling and drifted silently among the floes until the bow of our kayak tapped one. On it, a seal was sound asleep. It opened its eyes, focused and blinked. Then our presence registered. With a "Holy Smokes!" look in its eyes, it squealed, slid off the ice and dove.

Later, we were startled ourselves by a powerful, ominous snort coming from behind. We spun around and stared into the eyes of three Steller sea lions. We weren't much good for eating, mating or picking a fight, they must have decided. Another snort and they were gone.

> They also say that in time the Sound will recover. But I don't believe it will ever be the same, at least not in my lifetime.

I've never known a place as rich as the Sound. I'm left with many more memories: Poking along wild beaches looking for sunbleached bones, feathers, shells and other treasures from the sea. Watching sea otters eat. Staring into a tidal pool as communities of invertebrates went about their subtle business. I must admit, I can't think of much I'd rather do.

Scientists have said the oil will become embedded in gravel beaches and slowly dispense toxins for years to come. They also say that in time the Sound will recover. But I don't believe it will ever be the same, at least not in my lifetime. Along with the countless birds, otters and other casualties of the spill, a part of me has died.

> 'It just tears me up. I feel like a person I've been close to has died.'

The following people have spent large portions of their lives in Prince William Sound. In the three weeks following the largest oil spill in U.S. history, they took time to remember the way it was.

Neil Johannsen, State Parks Director

"The only thing that's going to heal Prince William Sound and the souls of Alaskans is time," said Neil Johannsen, state parks director and author of a guidebook to the Sound. "It just tears me up. I feel like a person I've been close to has died."

Johannsen began exploring the Sound in 1973 aboard the 30 foot sloop Nellie Juan. He'd spend up to a month at a time sailing from cove to cove, dropping shrimp pots, fishing for salmon and flounder and never seeing another human for days on end.

His most cherished experiences include the sounds he heard one night in Jackpot Bay when it was too dark to see. First, he heard a whale blow while he was sailing through the entrance of the bay. When he dropped his anchor, he could hear salmon splashing in a stream near shore. When he struck a match to light a lantern, the flash startled a bear prowling on the beach, and it crashed through the woods in a panic. Johannsen considers this night a statement of the richness of Prince William Sound.

Johannsen met Prince William Sound resident George Flemming in the summer of 1974. A storm had settled in, pinning him on Knight Island, where Flemming was tending a turn-of-the-century herring saltery. A halibut boat was tied up there, too, and the fishermen hauled ashore slabs of fresh fish. The group feasted and passed around a whiskey bottle while one of the fishermen played Bach on an old piano by lantern light.

"We just had a rousing time that night," Johannsen said.

Flemming grew up on the Sound. He was born in 1905 in a log cabin on an island named for his father at the northern end of Prince of Wales Passage. His father was a whaler, his mother a Chugach Eskimo. The family ran a fox farm on Flemming Island.

Johannsen recalls standing on the deck of the Nellie Juan in the rain, pulling sails out of a bag, going on and on about how fast the world was changing. Flemming listened politely, then mentioned he hadn't been to town since 1930.

Johannsen was floored. Are you serious? He started telling him about how much Anchorage had grown. He talked about the freeways, the highrises, the way everybody's in such a big hurry. "You just wouldn't believe," he said.

"Neil," Flemming said. "I've never been to Anchorage. I was talking about Cordova."

Flemming died about five years ago. His ashes are scattered on the island where he grew up. When oil started moving in that direction, Johannsen's heart began to break.

"He loved that place so much . . . and now it's oiled."

"I can't shake the grief I feel over Prince William Sound," Johannsen said. "I have to let it in in small pieces.

I can't let it in my heart all at once. I don't think I could function."

Woods become parking lots, game trails become freeways, farms become subdivisions. As Johannsen sees it, change that happens slowly is called progress. When it happens quickly, it's called a disaster. But the result is the same: wildlife killed, habitat ruined.

He said he hopes the oil spill will strengthen environmental ethics.

"If it doesn't do that, then I'm afraid the oil spill has been a double tragedy."

R.J. Kopchak, Fisherman

Fisherman R.J. Kopchak has paid his dues. He arrived in Cordova in 1974 with nothing, camping out that first season in a boat in dry dock. After years of crewing for others, he finally bought his own gill netting permit. Last year, he and his wife, Barclay, finished building a stunning Victorian-style house that overlooks the boat harbor.

This was going to be the summer everything went smoothly, Kopchak says. He had a good season last year. The house was finished. He'd have some time to work on his boat.

After fishing Prince William Sound for 16 years, you'd think it would be difficult to pinpoint the best memory. For Kopchak, it wasn't the biggest haul; it was the year his first child was born.

He took time off from fishing to help deliver his baby. His daughter, Sager, was only two weeks old when he bundled her up and took her fishing with him in Coghill District in College Fjord, in the northern part of the Sound. She slept on the driver's seat in a canned salmon box while Kopchak and his wife shared the day bunk.

One of his second child's first words was "whale." The family had finished up at Coghill and had taken a trip across the Sound to the San Juan hatchery. On the way back home, during a leisurely drive past Knight Island, the Kopchaks came upon a pod of 18 to 20 orcas. They spent half the day watching the whales rising out of the water and splashing back down again. Whenever a whale would blow, Zachariah would yell, "Whale!"

> 'Now our whole lifestyle has changed. . . . Just from being from the Sound, fish are tainted fish, in many people's eyes.'

This is why Kopchak chose to be a fisherman. He wanted work that he could do with his family.

"All of my kids fished before they could walk," he said. Zachariah learned to crawl on the deck of the boat. The third child, Obadiah, learned to crawl on Knight Island just last year.

"I flew over that beach," Kopchak said. "It's black with tar now. It is a dead zone in that portion of the Sound."

Their fourth child is due in October. Kopchak said he's sorry this one won't be able to know the Sound as it used to be.

"Now our whole lifestyle has changed," he said. "Just from being from the Sound, fish are tainted fish, in many people's eyes. There's not an untouched family here. It's a loss of innocence."

And Cordova has become a different town.

"All we want to be here is plain, simple fishing people. We have been invaded."

Still, life goes on. The Copper River Flats should open for salmon fishing as usual, Kopchak said. "The Copper River reds are in beautiful shape . . . (the flats) are a long way from where this happened.

"This has changed me as a person . . . it just brought home how incredibly fragile everything is.

"But I will come out the other end, and Cordova in general will come out the other end as better and stronger people. But I wish I could have just skipped it, OK?"

Kelly Weaverling and Susan Ogle

Kelley Weaverling arrived in Prince William Sound 13 years ago by floatplane, after wandering the world in search of a place to stay. The problem was, he missed the mountains when he was on the sea, and missed the sea when he was in the mountains. He didn't realize he could have it both ways.

As the plane flew off, Weaverling assembled his collapsible kayak on the shore of Port Nellie Juan's Derickson Bay. He looked around.

Mountains rose to the sky and glaciers calved into the sea. Sea otters and seals peeked at him from the water's surface and from atop ice floes. A pod of orcas swam by, including one with a crooked dorsal fin that he named Bent Fin and has seen every year since.

"I realized, this is it. I'm home. This is paradise. I'm going to spend the rest of my life in Prince William Sound."

Weaverling and his wife, Susan Ogle, spent five summers in the Sound guiding with Bear Brothers kayak tours, and another five summers exploring the Sound on their own, working now and then as natural history consultants for the National Outdoor Leadership School.

Two years ago they decided they wanted to live on the Sound year-round. They moved from Anchorage to Cordova and bought a bookstore and a house within walking distance of the shore.

Among their most prized possessions is knowledge of a beach frequented by killer whales. They discovered it by accident, while camped on a steep beach covered with smooth pebbles. They were startled late one night by the eerie sound of whales spouting. They peeked out of their tent and saw seven orcas, Bent Fin among them, headed their way. And they didn't stop.

'I have a journal filled with 10 years of special moments. . . . Now, unfortunately, the ending is very apparent.'

The whales swam up onto the beach until they were half out of the water. Then they began to rub, inching along sideways, scratching first their bellies, then their sides. They kept this up for 15 minutes, then wiggled back into the water and swam away.

Weaverling and Ogle have no idea what's happened to Bent Fin or the rest of the resident orcas they feel they know. They're not sure they want to.

"I have a journal filled with 10 years of special moments," Ogle said. "I thought it would make a great book, but it didn't have an ending. I thought maybe the ending would be moving to Cordova and living happily ever after. Now, unfortunately, the ending is very apparent."

Since the accident, Ogle has been working as the spill response coordinator for Cordova. Weaverling is working with the wildlife rescue people in Valdez and has organized a fleet of Cordova fishermen to pick up oiled animals and birds.

He also has been trying to set up a sea otter rescue center in Cordova. But . . . U.S. Fish and Wildlife officials informed him that without a special permit, picking up sea otters was a violation of the federal Marine Mammal Protection Act.

"I was so low, you could have run over me with a snake," Weaverling said. "I just crawled off."

He's back now, rescuing what he can: birds only. He wears a black arm band, a symbol of mourning.

The Captain of the *Exxon Valdez* Describes the Spill and Its Aftermath

Joseph Hazelwood

In the following viewpoint, the captain of the *Exxon Valdez* gives his perspective of when the tanker ran aground and spilled oil into Prince William Sound. He briefly discusses the events leading up to the disaster and then describes the period after the spill, when he was hounded by reporters and nationally vilified. He talks about his trial, which, after multiple appeals, resulted in a conviction, including a fine and community service. He concludes by acknowledging that as captain he was responsible for the spill, and he offers his apologies to the people of Alaska.

SOURCE. Joseph Hazelwood, "Joseph Hazelwood, Captain of the *Exxon Valdez*," *The Spill: Personal Stories from the Exxon Valdez Disaster*, ed. Stan Jones and Sharon Bushell, Epicenter Press, 2009. Copyright © 2009 Epicenter Press. Inc. All rights reserved. Reproduced by permission.

The day of March 23rd [1989], I had some ship's business to attend to, as did the chief engineer. On my list was to order flowers for my daughter, which I always did every Easter. If I hadn't had any pressing business I probably wouldn't have gone ashore. I had no burning desire to go to Valdez. At any rate, the chief engineer and I went to town around eleven in the morning. After lunch we had a couple of drinks.

> Everyone behaved professionally. . . . For all of us [running aground] was an alien situation.

The Safety of the Crew was Paramount

After the grounding, the safety of the crew was paramount, as was the safety of the ship, and retaining safely the cargo that was still left on board. As for the cargo that had escaped, we weren't going to get that back. We were trying to maintain the structural integrity of the ship as it was on the rocks.

Everyone behaved professionally, but of course they were a little uptight. For all of us it was an alien situation.

A couple hours later, when the first two Coast Guard officers got to the *Exxon Valdez*, they asked me what the problem was. I told them, "You're looking at it," by which I meant that the ship was on the rocks and a huge amount of oil was leaking. It was a comment that was widely misinterpreted.

When Captain [William] Deppe arrived at nine or ten in the evening on Friday, we had a change of command. I told him as much as I knew. I had the pilot boat take some soundings around the vessel so we knew what the depth of the water was adjacent to the ship and the condition of the tanks. At the same time, the *Baton Rouge* was coming alongside to lighter the vessel. Captain Deppe then gave me the keys to a room in the Sheffield

Hotel. The place was mobbed with people coming and going and no one took any notice of me.

I met with the NTSB [National Transportation Safety Board] in Valdez [Alaska] and told them I wasn't going to speak to them. Then I left. That was a choice I made based on some advice my father had given me years earlier. He had been an airplane pilot who had had some involvement with the NTSB, and his thought was that no good had come from dealing with them.

> I'd glance at a newspaper, see my face, and think, 'Boy, that guy's really in trouble.'

I returned to New York. . . .

The Aftermath and Trial

It was good to get back to familiar surroundings, but my house was under siege. There were three news trucks parked in the front yard and reporters all over the lawn, in the back yard and on the porches. They were stealing the garbage and stealing the mail. One of my neighbors worked for the postal service. He called the marshals in to put a stop to that, as they were stealing his garbage, too. That commotion lasted for about two weeks, during which time my family and I temporarily moved to another house.

That first year was really rocky and I found myself living my life—parts of it—in third person. I'd glance at a newspaper, see my face, and think, "Boy, that guy's really in trouble." I assume it was some kind of defense mechanism that kicked in in my psyche. I didn't do it consciously, but it seemed to work.

To a certain degree, that first year, I was stalked, but after that I was no longer recognized. Occasionally there was some name recognition, but no physical recognition that I was aware of.

Most important to me was that my family and friends didn't think any less of me; that was the thing that mattered most. I was thrust into the spotlight for a while but I was still a private person, and the people closest to me never wavered in their support.

The criminal justice process involved a couple of trips back to Alaska for arraignments. There I pled not guilty and returned home, then I returned to Alaska for subsequent charges and pled not guilty to those as well.

There was a whole procedure of motions and discovery, and then the actual trial commenced in late January of 1990. That went on for seven or eight weeks, then there was a verdict. I was acquitted of three out of the four charges, with one misdemeanor count remaining. There was a sentencing: $50,000 and 1,000 hours of community service, then there was an appeals process. The remaining charge was thrown out on appeal twice. Finally the Alaska Supreme Court sustained it, and that

Joseph Hazelwood, former captain of the *Exxon Valdez*, was ordered to perform one thousand hours of community service. Hazelwood prepared meals at Bean's Café, an Anchorage organization that provides free meals to the homeless, to fulfill his obligations. (**AP Images/Al Grillo.**)

was the end of the appeals. Then the sentence, which had been stayed until the appeals were exhausted, was imposed.

Surprisingly, during the trial very few people said unkind things about me, except for the prosecutor. For the most part, the witnesses did not. Things were pretty low key. There were no histrionics or Perry Mason moments. It was pretty straightforward. Intellectually, it was interesting, except for the fact that I was the defendant.

The prosecution had subpoenaed the ship's crew and they were truthful in their testimony. I do want to say, I got to know one of the courtroom reporters pretty well, the lead crime reporter for the AP, Linda Deutsch. When the prosecution rested she made the offhand comment, "Are they going to bother to prove anything?" Her next question was, "Are you going to bother to put in a defense, because the prosecution hasn't proven anything?"

The true story is out there for anybody who wants to look at the facts, but that's not the sexy story and that's not the easy story. People want to hear the news when they want it, and they don't want to delve into any complicated thought processes. They'll settle for quick sound bites. That's what happened and we'll leave it at that.

I don't know if I'm hardwired this way, but I've never been a whiner. I've never thought it accomplished much. There are a lot of people in this world with a lot of problems, and I've got a few myself. But I don't think there's any sense in belaboring your troubles. I've always felt that if you've got animosity or distaste for something, you have to personalize it somehow. It's tough to hate a corporation, and Exxon is a very big corporation. I was able to give a personal name for people who, for lack of a better term, needed to vent their spleens.

I don't have any particular animosity toward Exxon. They had great ships, and they paid me well for a job that I loved doing. They were a good corporation to work for.

Of course, I had differences with them over the years, which every employee has with every employer, but nothing that couldn't be overcome between adults.

As for community service, I started off by picking up trash along the Anchorage roads. That only lasted one day because the director of community services in Anchorage, as he put it, really didn't want me out on the street somewhere, tying up traffic with people ogling me in an orange jumpsuit.

By the time I returned that first day, my lawyer and the head of community service had called around and found that Bean's Café [an Anchorage institution that provides fee meals to the homeless] was always looking for able bodies to help out. We met with the director of Bean's and he said sure, come on and work for us. It was a little bit overkill when I first started there. There were three satellite trucks in the parking lot, which I thought was a bit much. But by the second or third time I went up there, I just came and went. I was old news.

> I was the captain of a ship that ran aground and caused a horrendous amount of damage. I've got to be responsible for that.

I worked at Bean's for three stints of five weeks each. I'd punch in in the morning at about five-thirty and punch out at around six o'clock at night, seven days a week. I did janitorial and maintenance work, cleaning stoves and grease pits, waxing floors, all kinds of things. One year we built an office. I have a little knowledge of computers, and Bean's had a bunch of donated computers, so I set them up one year.

Apologizing to Alaska

Nowadays, I do some investigations and consulting on technical issues for a maritime law firm in New York. I've always enjoyed to sail, and I get on the water as much as I can. I don't own any sailboats now but I sail for other people on occasion. Most of the racing we do in the summer season is in Long Island Sound, and some off-shore racing down in Bermuda. In the spring, I'll bring yachts up to the Northeast from Florida and the Caribbean and then take them down in the fall.

After the oil spill, looking at the upside, the biggest thing for me was that I got to know my daughter a little better in some of her more formative years: junior high, high school, and college, which I probably wouldn't have normally because I would have been gone half the time. She is a very strong kid and all her friends were supportive of her. The biggest event for her was when the reporters found out what school she was in.

They all gathered at her school to try to get her to make a statement for them. God only knows why. My neighbor was a New York state trooper. His daughter was a good friend of my daughter's. When this incident happened, the friend called her father. It just happened to be his day off, so he slapped on his uniform and chased the reporters off the school grounds. The administration didn't really know what to do, so he just took it upon himself to do a little proactive crowd control.

Another positive thing was that I met a lot of nice people that I would never have met otherwise. Of course, I would rather have met them a little more on my own terms. Prior to the spill, I always enjoyed meeting Alaskans. They seemed very genuine, and I admire their independent spirit. After the Valdez spill, I never had any problems with the people of Alaska. I always felt that they gave me a fair shake.

Occasionally people have called me a scapegoat, but I've never felt comfortable with that term when applied to me in regard to the oil spill. I was the captain of a ship that ran aground and caused a horrendous amount of damage. I've got to be responsible for that. There's no way around it. Some of the things that came later, the efforts at cleaning up, were really beyond my purview, but it still goes back to that: if my ship hadn't run aground and spilled part of its cargo, the event never would have happened.

I can't escape that responsibility, nor do I want to. I would like to offer an apology, a very heartfelt apology, to the people of Alaska for the damage caused by the grounding of a ship that I was in command of.

Alaska Natives React to Oil Industry Pollution

Winona LaDuke

In the following viewpoint, an activist discusses the concerns of Alaska Natives about oil industry pollution years after the *Exxon Valdez* oil spill. Communities have gathered together to form the Alaska Native Oil and Gas Working Group and challenge the oil industry in Alaska and surrounding Alaska Native Corporations. They feel that these industries and corporations intend to exploit the land and resources that are available for the use of the indigenous people. The Alaska Natives state that it is crucial for the natural resources to be uncontaminated for their continued use, and that studies have shown high amounts of toxins contaminating fisheries and other traditional resources, making them unsafe for use. Winona LaDuke is a Native rights activist and was Ralph Nader's running mate on the Green Party ticket in the 2000 presidential election.

SOURCE. Winona LaDuke, "Alaska: Oil and the Natives," *Earth Island Journal*, Autumn 2003, p. 30(2). Reproduced by permission.

It's 14 years since the *Exxon Valdez* oil spill in Alaska. The oil industry still drives the state's politics and much of the environment. Senator Frank Murkowski has just been elected governor, and has appointed his daughter to fill out his term in the Senate. Linda Murkowski is proposing a bill that would exempt most new oil exploitation from any environmental impact statements. Meanwhile, Prince William Sound is still not cleaned up. Of the 28 species most affected by the spill, only two are on the recovery list.

"It will be a long time until we know the damages to our way of life," explains Dune Lankard. Lankard, of the Eyak community of Cordova; Evon Peter, Chief of the Gwich'in Nation from Arctic Village; and Violet Yeaton, from Port Graham Village on Lower Cook Inlet, have joined hundreds of other Alaska Natives to form the Alaska Native Oil and Gas Working Group. They are challenging the oil industry in Alaska, the sacred cow of Alaskan politics. They're also challenging the activities of the Alaska Native Corporations, which, they charge, were created as tools to exploit the lands and resources of indigenous people.

> "Though visually stunning, Alaska . . . is the fourth most polluted state in the country."

Grassroots Community Groups Address Environmental Damage

Concerns over unsustainable oil and gas development, with its attendant environmental and cultural impacts on Alaska Natives, prompted grassroots community groups to form the Working Group. The process was supported by international organizations such as Project Underground and the Indigenous Environmental Network through the Indigenous Mining Campaign.

"Our traditional use [of natural resources] in an uncontaminated state is crucial to the sustainability of our culture," says Yeaton. "We require zero discharge."

Studies have documented heavy metals and persistent organic pollutants contaminating fisheries and other traditional resources. One such study was conducted by the EPA [Environmental Protection Agency]. Before the final report was completed, the EPA renewed permits for local oil and gas development based on exemptions from the law, exemptions that are illegal elsewhere. . . .

Robert Thompson, an Inupiat from Kaktovi—a village with a long history of involvement in oil development—admits that many people in his area support oil development. Nonetheless, he sees a threat to native ways of life from the oil industry. "The Porcupine caribou herd is in decline. There are no safeguards during the production stage of oil and gas. [The herd is] having problems without any development . . . development will further damage this herd." Thompson's goal is to forestall that damage, and to preserve the caribou for the future. "It is my hope that the seventh generation will come to know our land and culture."

Oil drove the transformation of Alaska, as well as the creation of the Alaskan Native Claims Settlement Act (ANCSA), which separated many Alaska Natives from jurisdiction over their land. Gwich'in Chief Evon Peter is blunt in his assessment of ANCSA: "[It] took nearly all the land from indigenous control and allowed the industry and state to gain access to the resources. It set up a tool to divide and exploit the Alaskan indigenous nations, their traditional lands, and resources."

Removal of the Natives' Claims to Their Land

When Alaska became the 49th state in 1959, about 85,000 Native people lived there. The discovery of oil prompted the federal government to address aboriginal title questions in the region, in order to find a tenable legal loophole through which to secure an 800-mile pipeline from the North Slope to Valdez.

That legal loophole was ANCSA. In 1971, the government set out to address the problem of Alaska Native jurisdiction. As Clayton Thomas-Muller of the Indigenous Environmental Network explains, "President [Richard] Nixon convinced Wally Hickel to retire as Governor of Alaska to be appointed Secretary of the Interior, making him instrumental in brokering the Alaskan Native Claims Settlement Act. With the passage of the ANCSA legislation, all aboriginal land claims were extinguished. The law passed without a vote by Alaska Native people or the general public." Native lands were given to for-profit Alaska Native Corporations, and the people were made shareholders. This was not so different from the "termination era," which liquidated the assets of many native communities in the lower 48. The law wreaked social havoc on Alaska Native communities.

Today, Alaska Native Corporations control huge tracts of land. The Chugach Alaska Corporation controls 930,000 acres. Cook Inlet Regional Corporation controls 2.4 million acres, and Nana Regional Corporation controls 2.25 million acres. Many of the corporations have entered into joint ventures or partnerships with mining and oil development companies. The Arctic Slope Regional Corporation (ASRC) holds entitlements to 5.1 million acres of land, including some lands rich in oil and minerals. Though 9 percent of the jobs are held by shareholders, ASRC's interests and responsibilities now include business partners like BP Amoco, which caused one of the region's largest crude oil spills. ASRC has caused its own spills as well, including one in February 2002 of more than 5,000 gallons of oil.

Addressing Pollution to Maintain a Way of Life

Though visually stunning, Alaska remains amazingly polluted. It's the fourth most polluted state in the country,

> "Oil exploration and production facilities, pipelines, and natural gas refirenies are exempted from [pollution] reporting requirements."

with over 535 million pounds of toxic releases into the environment in 2000 alone. One lead and zinc mine, the Red Dog Mine in the Nana Regional Corporation's territory, reported 450 million pounds of toxic releases in 2000, or about four-fifths of all reported toxic releases in the state. There is significant controversy about pollution from the mine, which employs many native people.

Oil exploration and production facilities, pipelines, and natural gas refineries are exempted from Toxics Release Inventory (TRI) reporting requirements. Despite the exemptions, Alaskan industry reported releases of 265,000 pounds of toxics from the oil facilities in 2000.

That same year, there were 1,534 oil spills in the state reported to the Alaska Department of Environmental Conservation. That amounts to a reported release of 145,338 gallons of oil, or 30 oil spills a week, four a day. In 2001, a spill was caused when 37-year-old Daniel Carson Lewis shot a hole in the Trans-Alaska Pipeline, spilling an estimated 6,800 barrels. From 1994 to 1999, according to one report, approximately 1,600 spills occurred involving more than 1.2 million gallons of oil, diesel fuel, acids, ethylene glycol, drilling fluid, produced water (brine from deep wells) and other liquids. A study of diesel spills in Alaska's Arctic region found that substantial hydrocarbons remained in the soil for up to 28 years, and vegetation in the spill areas had not recovered.

Industry representatives justify the pollution reporting exemption by saying that the facilities are located too far from communities to have an impact. However, for Violet Yeaton, Evon Peter, or Dune Lankard's communities, that exemption has proved problematic.

"The Chugach Alaska Corporation has decided it wants to drill for oil near Katalla, on the Copper River

Delta and an ancestral village site of the Eyak," points out Lankard, whose Indian name means "a little bird who screams really loud and won't shut up." "We've never been asked for our opinion. The Copper River Delta is home to the world's finest salmon, and we do not want to lose this way of life. If the development happens at Katalla, it will affect everything we know about the Copper River Delta."

The Alaska Native Oil and Gas Working Group promises not only to challenge major oil companies over new Alaskan oil exploitation proposals, but to push Native Corporations and the state of Alaska to diversify the region's economy, while addressing the pollutants already dispersed throughout Alaska. The challenge is immense; Peter, Lankard, Yeaton and their colleagues are in for a long campaign.

An Activist Discusses Her Town's Reaction to the Disaster

Riki Ott

In the following viewpoint, a local woman discusses her experiences in Cordova, Alaska, in the days and months following the *Exxon Valdez* spill. She notes that the people of Cordova were angry at Exxon and fearful for the environment and their own livelihoods. The influx of money from Exxon, she reports, caused major disruptions in daily life, and the stresses caused by the spill and its aftermath affected the townspeople for many years. Riki Ott is a community activist, a former commercial salmon fisherman, and a marine toxicologist.

SOURCE. Riki Ott, *Not One Drop: Betrayal and Courage in the Wake of the Exxon Valdez Spill*, Chelsea Green Publishing, 2008. Copyright © 2008 Chelsea Green Publishing. All rights reserved. Reproduced by permission.

On the afternoon of March 28 [1989], Jack Lamb and I and some others flew to Cordova [Alaska, a town near the oil spill] to attend the town meeting. We found the community engulfed in chaos. It was Cordova's darkest hour. The shock of the spill had worn off. People despaired openly in the streets. People knew this spill threatened the entire town because everyone was linked like a big daisy chain to commercial fishing and the Sound [Prince William Sound]. Fish bucks drove the economy and, without fish, there would be no bucks.

Anger at Exxon

Nearly 2,000 angry, adrenaline-charged people showed up at the high school gym for the town meeting. The crowd hissed at the sweeping promises Exxon's Don Cornett flung to appease us. "You have had some good luck and you don't realize it. You don't have the *Glacier Bay* [a ship that spilled oil in Alaska in 1987], you have Exxon and we do business straight. . . . We will consider whatever it takes to make you whole. . . . If your nets don't fill up, that we can take care of. If you show that your motel goes out of business, that we can take care of. . . . If you can show that you have a loss as a result of this spill, we will compensate it. . . ." Cornett also promised Exxon would clean each rock with a toothbrush, if necessary.

> Many . . . remembered when oilmen had visited the town during the pre-pipeline days and had promised there would be no big spills.

Cordovans listened, unbelieving. Many sitting in the gym remembered when oilmen had visited the town during the pre-pipeline days and had promised there would be no big spills. And if there were, the oilmen could quickly and efficiently clean them up. Now it was painfully obvious neither statement was true. The oilmen couldn't even begin to comprehend what we had lost.

Motels and fishing businesses! What about our lifestyle? The Natives' subsistence foods? Our beautiful Sound?

The next day, I found the CDFU [Cordova District Fishermen United] office had transformed in my five-day absence into a madhouse. There were five phone lines, four desks, and a dozen volunteers at any given time, all operating out of the tiny office. Volunteers found and acquired boom—industrial heavy-weather boom, not Alyeska's[1] "mill pond" boom, as the fishermen called it. They hired and dispatched boats to the cleanup; coordinated efforts with the hatcheries; took donations; screened calls from hundreds of attorneys and "miracle cure" beach-cleaning-product salesmen; made overflights; dealt with constant calls from media around the world; talked with thousands of people who called just to help; met with the state, NOAA [National Oceanic and Atmospheric Administration] scientists, the Coast Guard, environmental groups, and other fishing organizations; and, most importantly, coordinated with the new CDFU office in Valdez. CDFU's phone lines were constantly jammed because the entire community's phone network was overloaded.

> Fishermen could use the spill as political leverage to push for safeguards that we had lost or had not been able to pass into law because of the powerful oil industry lobby.

CDFU had broad community support. The union hall outside the office became a gathering place to catch up on the news. Bakery-store owners brought trays of doughnuts in the morning, and bread and cold cuts at noon. In the evening, families brought entire roast turkeys, trays of lasagna, pots of spaghetti, and home-baked cookies. Children decorated the walls with whimsical creatures in colorful collages and crude crayon drawings of the Sound they loved. Preschoolers offered finger paintings of "helping hands." Donated dog kennels for the wildlife rescue efforts, temporary stockpiles of boom, and boxes of absorbent pads were stacked from floor to ceiling.

Theo Matthews, president of United Fishermen of Alaska [UFA] and a survivor of the *Glacier Bay* oil spill, had joined us in Valdez to help with strategy. "You know," he had said, "if this oil spill gets out of Prince William Sound, it's comin' straight to Cook Inlet."

The Spill as an Opportunity

Now in Cordova, Theo took one look at the CDFU office with its overwhelming noise and energy level and pulled me out into the street. "Look, there are enough people getting equipment and boats organized. I want you to find somewhere quiet, sit down, and use your brain and your computer. We need someone to think up ideas for the politicians in D.C. so we're ready when they start working on spill legislation." Theo realized fishermen could use the spill as political leverage to push for safeguards that we had lost or had not been able to pass into law because of the powerful oil industry lobby. When he saw I had a quiet place to stay and work in town, he went home. "Call me any time of the day or night, darlin'. Good luck!"

For three weeks, I pulled fifteen- to eighteen-hour days researching and writing; talking with press, scientists, and attorneys; and attending daily CDFU board meetings to deal with issues of shoreline cleanup, media logistics, state and federal legislation, damage claims, and lawsuits. It was like cramming for final exams at the university, only the stakes were higher. Congressmen and U.S. Senators who were aloof and distant to the UFA delegation during our February visit called repeatedly for information.

In mid-April, CDFU sent Michelle Hahn O'Leary and me to Washington, D.C. to testify. The homework Theo Matthews had me do paid off. I spoke to politicians with a headful of figures and a fistful of documents, while Michelle addressed the failed spill response. Our work helped frame legislation for the Oil Pollution Act of 1990.

Michelle and I raced back to Cordova just in time to celebrate Sound Love Day with our community. Huge brightly colored murals made by elementary schoolchildren decorated the high school gym. One of the town's favorite musicians, folksinger and songwriter John McCutcheon, came cross-country to help shift the sadness and grief. We wore red hearts on our sleeves and celebrated our love with spontaneous song, statements, silence, prayers, and poems. Buoyed by the atmosphere of trust and sharing, one small child told the crowd of 2,000, "Boat captains should drink milk." Sound Love Day was a psychological turning point for the community. It was a powerful emotional pickup of affirmation and commitment to each other and the Sound. Memories of this day would help townspeople endure what lay ahead.

Sound Love Day drew people from around the world. Jonathan Wills, a reporter with the *Shetland Times* in Scotland, came to write a story comparing operations at the Alyeska terminal with its sister terminal at Sullom Voe, half a world away, also owned primarily by BP.[2] Amazed by Alyeska's lack of spill response preparation and by the government's lack of control over oil industry operations, Jonathan crossed the line between correspondent and participant. He shared his wealth of information with CDFU and others. According to Jonathan, people in Shetland—sheep ranchers and farmers in rural communities not much bigger than Cordova—had demanded and been given a significant role in oversight. Shetlanders had wielded this power to gain significant improvements in tanker and terminal operations. We seized Jonathan's information like drowning victims seize life rings.

Danny [Carpenter, Ott's partner] arrived shortly after Sound Love Day. Unable to reach me on March 24, he

Photo on following page: Local residents of Cordova, Alaska, were paid high wages to help clean up oil after the *Exxon Valdez* spill, causing severe labor shortages elsewhere in Cordova's economy. (AP Images/ John Gaps III.)

> Most townspeople suspected Exxon's cleanup was a public relations effort, not an honest attempt to clean up oil.

had turned on the television—and there I was. Brokenhearted by oiled images of the Sound and with no stomach for politics, he had delayed his return. While Danny readied our boat and gear for fishing, I bounced across the country, testifying at congressional hearings, attending meetings, and dealing with the crush of media during the preseason time we normally spent together. . . .

"Should we work the cleanup?" It was a question I felt obligated to ask Danny. Some fishermen had already made a season's income before the salmon fishing had even started. To my enormous relief, he replied flatly, "*Amber-gris* is a fishing boat, not an oil spill cleanup boat."

Exxon Money Hurts the Community

For us, it was not a hard decision to make or to live with, but about one-third of the fleet worked on the cleanup. The spill had closed the herring fisheries in the Sound and would certainly impact the salmon fisheries. Lawyers advised people to "mitigate their damages" by taking cleanup contracts. Many fishermen reasoned they needed the work to pay home mortgages, boat and permit loans, living expenses, and other bills.

Exxon's contracts were extremely lucrative, but the cleanup program had started out badly. After the successful community-driven effort to protect Sawmill Bay, Exxon assumed full control of the cleanup. The required contracts for fishermen had initially banned personal cameras on the cleanup, boats from transporting press, and contractors from even talking to media. Most townspeople suspected Exxon's cleanup was a public relations effort, not an honest attempt to clean up oil. Part of this was driven by people who had gone to work the cleanup with good intentions, but who had returned sickened and with firsthand stories of the charade. After all, Tom Copeland and his crew on the *Janice N* collected more oil in one day with five-gallon buckets than Exxon with its fancy skimmers.

The ensuing moral debate over whether or not to accept Exxon's money for cleanup work eroded social solidarity. Families argued about it. Friendships shattered over it. The debate even spilled into CDFU meetings, where the board was bitterly divided over whether to ask Exxon for compensation for hundreds of extra hours for meetings that consumed our lives. Charges of favoritism and bribery were rampant as people vied for the lucrative spill contracts. Many believed that Exxon purposefully created divisiveness within the community by selective hire practices and by inequitable pay for similar services to prevent a concerted effort from forming against it. Exxon's money spill shattered what little sanity there was left in town. The weight of it crushed our civil society.

Exxon's pay of $16.69 per hour with overtime also drew Cordova's labor force like moths to a flame. The mass exodus to the Sound crippled the ability of the government and business community to function effectively. Employers were forced to raise wages, pay large amounts of overtime, shut down certain operations, or even close their doors. Processors lost about one-third of their workforce. "Our people . . . are starting to get restless as they see people around, even friends, who have already made a whole season's wages while our crew is just getting by," said one processor. "I can't compete with Exxon wages," grumbled a bar owner who lost two of his four employees. "It's a pit—I have to work sixteen hours a day, because I can't get help," said another employer who lost three of his four workers to the spill. "Our employees need three weeks' prior training. We can't just pick new people up off the street," said a fuel distributor who lost two of his six workers.

Those remaining in town carried the burden for all. There were thousands of decisions and hundreds of hours of volunteer work to hold the community and fishing fleet together. We moved from one crisis to another, hour after hour, day after day. Tempers strained; tensions were overwrought; people argued and fought; children were fearful and confused. The emotional havoc rippled from individuals to families to businesses until the entire town was overwhelmed by trauma. John Crowley, Director of the Mental Health and Alcohol Clinic in Cordova, reported a fivefold increase in the number of patients. Overworked mental health clinic staff couldn't even begin to plug the dike of fear, confusion, anger, and grief that spilled out when conflicts, domestic violence, and drinking skyrocketed. No one knew that these ripples of social chaos would outlast the cleanup by decades.

> When the plane entered the spill zone and flew on and on over blackened beaches, the enormity of the destruction sunk in and my mother started to cry.

Hearings in the Sound

In early May, my parents came to visit, as planned. Danny, kindhearted and generous with his time, was distraught. He loved my parents, but had no free time to spare. I assured him they were fully prepared to entertain themselves. They had hesitated to come after the spill, but I said, "The birds are still coming, so why shouldn't you?" They volunteered at the CDFU office and filled me in daily on cleanup stories. When I asked how they came by such detailed information, Dad said, "I make a general announcement at the little café in the bookstore—'We are Riki Ott's parents'—and all sorts of people come to talk with us!" Once they flew on the mail plane to the Native Village of Chenega. When the plane entered the spill zone and flew on and on over blackened beaches, the enormity of the destruction sunk in and my mother started to cry. The Native man sitting next to her quietly held her hand. "That made me cry even more," said Mom, "when I saw his home was surrounded by oil." They also attended the first annual Shorebird Festival, an event that the U.S. Forest Service and determined towns-people hosted in spite of the spill—and shared what I had missed.

Coinciding with my parents' visit, Congressman George Miller (D-CA) held a series of field hearings in the Sound. CDFU sent Jack Lamb, Ken Adams, and me to Valdez to testify. My parents flew with us. Before I testified, my father whispered, "Remember, in a public forum like this, never ask a question if you don't know the answer."

A panel of oilmen testified after us. Silver-haired, silver-tongued Theo Polasek, the vice president of Alyeska operations, defended its contingency plan, testifying that it "accurately portrayed what would happen in the case of a 200,000-barrel spill." This was the same contingency plan that ADEC [Alaska Department of Environmental Conservation] commissioner Denny Kelso had referred to earlier as "the biggest piece of American maritime fiction since Moby-Dick."

My father, watching Polasek intently, nudged me. He mocked an imaginary long nose like Pinocchio. "He's lying! Pink ears!" Listening to my father, I realized I still had a lot to learn.

Notes

1. The Alyeska Pipeline Service Company was the organization responsible for overseeing oil spill cleanups.
2. BP was the main oil company in control of Alyeska.

CHRONOLOGY

1989   March 23: The *Exxon Valdez* oil tanker departs the marine oil terminal in Valdez, Alaska, at 9:12 P.M., bound for California with 53 million gallons of crude oil.

March 24: The *Exxon Valdez* runs aground at approximately 12:04 A.M., spilling more than 11 million gallons of oil into the waters around Prince William Sound, Alaska.

March 25: Exxon assumes financial responsibility for the spill as well as control of cleanup efforts, relieving the Alyeska Pipeline Service Company of cleanup responsibility.

March 26: A severe winter storm disperses the oil.

March 28: Due to the storm, officials admit that the oil slick cannot not be contained. Emphasis is shifted to protecting sensitive areas.

March 29: The first beach cleanup crews are dispatched. Two fishermen file the first lawsuits against Exxon.

March 30: Joseph Hazelwood, the captain of the *Exxon Valdez*, is fired from the Exxon Shipping Company for drunkenness.

July: In accordance with an executive order by Alaska governor Steve Cowper, two tugboats begin to escort every tanker from Valdez out through Prince William Sound.

1990   March 23: Joseph Hazelwood is acquitted of felony charges but convicted of a misdemeanor for negligence for his role in grounding the *Exxon Valdez*. He is sentenced to perform one thousand hours of community service and fined $50,000.

August: The Oil Pollution Act of 1990 is signed by Congress in response to the *Exxon Valdez* spill. The law imposes liability for cleanup costs on companies, but also caps damages.

1991   October 9: A federal judge approves a financial settlement among the State of Alaska, the US government, and Exxon. Exxon is to pay $25 million to environmental groups, $50 million each to the state and the federal governments, and $900 million to restore wildlife populations and habitat.

1992   Cleanup operations end. The total cost of the cleanup is $2.2 billion.

1994   September 16: A jury in United States District Court awards punitive damages against Exxon in the amount of $5 billion, and against Captain Joseph Hazelwood in the amount of $5,000.

2006   December 22: An Appeals Court reduces Exxon's punitive damages by half, to $2.5 billion.

2008   June 25: The Supreme Court reduces Exxon's punitive damages from $2.5 billion to $500 million.

2010   April 20: The Deepwater Horizon drilling rig explodes in the Gulf of Mexico. Oil flows for three months from the broken well, eclipsing the *Exxon Valdez* as the largest oil spill in US history.

FOR FURTHER READING

Books

Bob Cavnar, *Disaster on the Horizon: High Stakes, High Risks, and the Story Behind the Deepwater Well Blowout*. White River Junction, VT: Chelsea Green Publishing Company, 2010.

Dyan daNapoli, *The Great Penguin Rescue: 40,000 Penguins, a Devastating Oil Spill, and the Inspiring Story of the World's Largest Animal Rescue*. New York: Free Press, 2010.

Mervin F. Fingas, *The Basics of Oil Spill Cleanup*, 2nd ed. Boca Raton, FL: CRC Press, 2000.

Robert Emmet Hernan, *This Borrowed Earth: Lessons from the Fifteen Worst Environmental Disasters Around the World*. New York: Palgrave MacMillan, 2010.

John Keeble and Natalie Fobes, *Out of the Channel: The Exxon Valdez Oil Spill in Prince William Sound*. Spokane: Eastern Washington University Press, 1999.

Riki Ott, *Sound Truth and Corporate Myths: The Legacy of the Exxon Valdez Oil Spill*. Cordova, AK: Dragonfly Sisters Press, 2005.

J. Steven Picou, Duane A. Gill, and Maurie J. Cohen, eds. *The Exxon Valdez Disaster: Readings on a Modern Social Problem*, 2nd edition. Los Altos, CA: Indo American Books, 2008.

Raymond Solly, *Nothing over the Side: Examining Safe Crude Oil Tankers*. Dunbeath, UK: Whitties Publishing, 2010.

Loren C. Steffy, *Drowning in Oil: BP and the Reckless Pursuit of Profit*. New York: McGraw-Hill, 2010.

Jeff Wheelwright, *Degrees of Disaster: Prince William Sound: How Nature Reels and Rebounds*. New Haven: Yale University Press, 1996.

Periodicals

Robert Barnes, "Justices Assess Financial Damages in Exxon Valdez Case," *Washington Post*, February 28, 2008. www.washingtonpost.com.

Sharon Begley, "How Quickly We Forget," *Newsweek*, May 7, 2010. www.newsweek.com.

Nancy Dillon, "Future Looks Bleak for Gulf: Alaska Still Hasn't Recovered from Exxon Valdez 21 Years Later," *New York Daily News*, June 20, 2010. www.nydailynews.com.

Economist, "In the Wake of the Exxon Valdez: The Devastating Impact of the Alaska Oil Spill," May 19, 1990.

Economist, "Inside the Empire of Exxon the Unloved," March 5, 1994.

Darren Goode, "Gulf Spill Raises Questions About Exxon Valdez Law," Salon, May 6, 2010. www.salon.com.

Sarah Graham, "Environmental Effects of *Exxon Valdez* Spill Still Being Felt," *Scientific American*, December 19, 2003. www.scientificamerican.com.

Steve Heyward, "We're Not Quitting Oil," The Corner—National Review Online, May 3, 2010. www.nationalreview.com.

Jason Linkins, "Exxon Valdez: How That Disaster Destroyed the Economy 20 Years Later," *Huffington Post*, August 6, 2010. www.huffingtonpost.com.

Eric Nalder, "Crude Deliveries Push Safety to the Limit," *Seattle Times*, November 12, 1989. http://seattletimes.nwsource.com.

New York Times, "Lessons of the Exxon Valdez," March 22, 2009. www.nytimes.com.

Dennis Nishi, "A Lifesaver for Birds in Distress," *Wall Street Journal*, May 11, 2010. http://online.wsj.com.

Natalie Phillips, "Oil Spill Scarred Otters," *Anchorage Daily News*, May 13, 1999. www.adn.com.

Bradford Plumer, "Is Cleaning Up an Oil Spill Impossible?" *New Republic*, May 10, 2010. www.tnr.com.

Seattle Times, "The Lost Frontier," September 24, 1989. http://seattletimes.nwsource.com.

Time, "Exxon Valdez: Joe's Bad Trip," July 24, 1989. www.time.com.

Bryan Walsh, "Still Digging Up *Exxon Valdez* Oil, 20 Years Later," *Time*, June 4, 2009. www.time.com.

Washington Post, "Exxon Valdez Skipper Breaks His Silence," May 13, 1994.

David Whitney, "Looking On Bright Side," *Anchorage Daily News*, May 13, 1999. www.adn.com.

William Yardley, "Recovery Still Incomplete After Valdez Spill," *New York Times*, May 5, 2010. www.nytimes.com.

Websites

Environmental Protection Agency, Office of Emergency Management (www.epa.gov/emergencies/index.htm). OEM is the government agency charged with preventing environmental accidents and responding to accidents when they occur. Its website (part of the larger EPA website) includes news releases, discussions of specific environmental laws and regulations, policy statements, and publications including annual reports. Its page specifically dealing with oil spills is http://www.epa.gov/oilspill.

***Exxon Valdez* Oil Spill Trustee Council** (www.evostc.state.ak.us). The *Exxon Valdez* Oil Spill Trustee Council is the body formed to oversee restoration of the injured ecosystem of Prince William Sound with the money obtained from Exxon through the civil settlement. Their website includes a broad range of documents, including annual status reports. It also includes updates on resources and services, notices of invitations for restoration proposals, and fact sheets for students, among other materials.

Hard Aground (www.adn.com/evos/pgs/intro.html). This is a website maintained by the *Anchorage Daily News*. It includes all of that newspaper's reporting on the *Exxon Valdez* disaster, from 1989 through 1998. Articles are organized chronologically and by theme, and are searchable by keyword. The site also includes images, maps, and a timeline.

INDEX

33 36